WHY HE'S DATING HER
(Instead of You)

WHY HE DIDN'T COMMIT, WHY HE LEFT, AND WHY YOU'RE STILL HOOKED

10 WAYS TO BE THE WOMAN EVERY MAN WANTS

Emilee Henderson

Why He's Dating Her
(Instead of You)

BY

EMILEE HENDERSON

For more information on this series, please visit us on the web at
10cups.com

ISBN 978-0-9818039-4-4

KRE, LLC
PO Box 121135
Nashville, TN 37212-1135

CONTENTS

Introduction

If you are a single woman who has ever wondered about how to make a relationship work over the long term, this book is for you. You may have no problem getting into a relationship, but soon enough those old, familiar nagging feelings resurface that tell you that you're doing something wrong, and yet each time you can't seem to pinpoint exactly which aspect of your relationship needs work—or what you can do about it.

Simply put, the secret to keeping the spark alive in a worthwhile long-term relationship is as easy as being able to recognize ten common dating mistakes and learn how they can be avoided or corrected. If you're open to heeding this life-changing advice, you'll be empowered with a new brand of self-confidence that will allow you to take on relationships without fear that you're somehow sabotaging your chances at lasting love.

Throughout your dating history, you may have asked yourself any number of the following questions:

- "Do I have to give up something for the sake of my relationship?"

- "Should I keep my relationship private from even my closest friends?"

- "When am I being too available?"

- "Will putting him on a pedestal help me cope with his personality?"

- "Do I need some kind of a personality overhaul to meet his requirements?"

- "Am I over-analyzing his actions? Does he really want a relationship with me?"

- "How can I keep my relationship from being split apart by traitorous friends?"

- "Where is Mr. Perfect? I want to meet him now!"

- "Where have all the quality guys gone? No one is good enough for me."

- "Do I need to take some time off from all these confusing relationship issues?"

After reading this book, you'll be able to understand and live your life in accordance with the key theme that runs through each chapter: Loving someone and building a successful and secure relationship all comes down to making the conscious choice to maintain a personal balance in your life and treating that balance in a sacred way.

Chapter 1: Never Lose Your Balance

even though it can feel like all of your efforts to attract a good man have paid off when you begin to get comfortable in a new relationship, the last thing you should do is stop focusing on the important things in your life that make you attractive to men—including your new boyfriend—in the first place. Women involved in the most successful long-term relationships know that it is not only possible to make time for your new relationship and balance your love life with your other interests, but it is also necessary for relationship longevity and positive self-health.

You can maintain that crucial balance between your new relationship and who you are by getting in tune with the common phases that all long-term relationships go through and making sure that you don't fall into common relationship traps.

THE HONEYMOON PHASE

New relationships are like a dream. You go from one date to another, spending most of your waking moments thinking about him, wondering when the next phone call, text message, or e-mail will come in. Every single day becomes a new page in your fairytale romance, where only the blossoming love between you matters. That magical quality makes the world spin on a very light and bright axis, and you are swept away by the tide of seemingly everlasting love.

The honeymoon phase is comfortable and fun, and it's so enjoyable living from one intense moment to the next that you might be hesitant to move on. But soon, the pressures of the real world you both temporarily left behind awaits—work commitments, family issues, and friends beckon you back, and it is only a matter of time before you must snap out of the fairytale and get back into ordinary life; this time, though, with the knowledge that you now have someone you could share it with.

THE FIRST CROSSROAD: THE PRIORITY TRAP

Have you ever felt compelled to give up an interest or a hobby for a man you love? Have you ever volunteered to give up your career so that you will have more time for him and your relationship? Have you ever felt that the opposite was true—that a man seems to have a hard time balancing his priorities with you?

The priority trap is real and it lurks around waiting for your relationship to reach that point where you both are pressed for time and seem to forget about meeting up for days or weeks. It is at this point that the feasibility of continuing the relationship may be questioned.

As a relationship progresses, one partner may continuously carve out large chunks of time to put toward the relationship that were previously devoted to other interests to make way for dates, love making, long lunches, and delightful afternoons together. Friends, team mates, colleagues and even bosses might cut them some slack initially because they are very happy for them. But for how long can they keep excluding individual responsibilities and priorities in favor of a budding relationship before feeling a deep sense of personal dissatisfaction creeps in? Both men and women may feel that relationships get in the way of successful careers or that their careers and other priorities prevent them from enjoying new relationships past the honeymoon phase.

The key to keeping a healthy balance between your individual life and relationship is to focus on one priority at a time and then devise ways to find balance with the new relationship. Juggling three-hour, lunchtime phone conversations and staying in touch from day to day throughout the week is a challenge, especially after enjoying so much undivided attention during their first months or weeks as lovers. In fact, the stress of balancing these two worlds can breed resentment, but if approached with a sense of balance, the relationship can continue to deepen while still meeting life's responsibilities.

Most of the time, a new relationship reaches its first crossroad when it's time to move on from the honeymoon phase when priorities become central issues. Time—or rather, the lack of it—seems to crop up more and more in conversations, and not in a positive way. There are many couples who get over this phase and are able to embrace life together, braving each day apart until they can meet up again, but there are also women, however, who decide to throw it all away.

ANNIE'S STORY (PART 1 OF 2)

Annie missed her new boyfriend; her first. They don't see each other as often as they did the summer before school started. She still goes to work in the café where they met, but this time she has to attend her classes at the local college. Being away from him and seeing him only sporadically during the week made her miserable. She soon quit her job and decided that she can handle college sometime soon in the future because what's important now is that she keeps seeing the guy who makes her so happy. Surely he'd love to spend more time with her, she reasons.

With a lot of free time on her hands to nurture the relationship now, she feels free. After class, she camps out at the park near his workplace to wait for him. They meet up every single day for a month, but then he started coming late, and sometimes not at all. She's baffled and hurt.

When she confronts him, she learns that he has taken a volunteer job, which entails showing a group of exchange students around for an hour or two each day. She feels hurt and frustrated that he dared take away some of their time together to help out other people. When she shared her feelings with him, she was aghast at the single sentence he uttered after she finished her tirade. "Don't you have other friends?"

Annie was unable to handle the pressure of being separated from her boyfriend because and felt that he would appreciate her devotion to him if she gave up something as important as her job for them to spend more time together. She also expected him to do the same; in the sense that he would put her over and above everything else. But Annie missed the most important point of relationship health: finding the crucial balance between her individual life and relationship life.

Meanwhile, her boyfriend's passion for helping other people and traits of selfless giving was lost on her because she could not see beyond the hurt she felt. His poignant question to her clearly indicates his concern about her lack of activities outside the relationship and that she seems to have him at the center of her world and nothing else—she is out of balance, and it shows in her obvious resentment about his other priorities and interests.

Let's delve into Annie's mind to get a better understanding of the priority trap. What made her quit a job she enjoyed for a new relationship? Is her mindset applicable for a lasting relationship?

Several stresses come into play just past the honeymoon stage. First, Annie realizes that inattention and lack of quality time together can break apart a relationship. To prevent that from happening, she rearranges her schedule in the name of love. Instead of sacrificing her own priorities right off the bat, it would have been better to shove the relationship in a spot inside her mental organizer and make room for it.

Second, she let her fears about non-relationship priorities come into play. Too scared of losing the relationship and not being able to pay for college, she risks the latter to be able to enjoy the former. Instead, it would have been better to weigh her priorities evenly, especially since college is very important to her.

Some women think that a man will appreciate them more if they show him that nothing in her life is more important than him. Burning bridges to make time for a new relationship reflects her idea of the relationship's lifespan, but some women don't think about the long term. They just want to be "in the moment," with their lives suspended in time to enjoy the romance without thinking of what will happen to her other relationships, opportunities, and interests.

Attention to a man is flattering, particularly when it's pouring like rain. But what happens when it doesn't let up? Won't a person feel overwhelmed and stifled by the attention? And what happens when that attention cannot be reciprocated?

One of the motives of a person who showers too much attention is to incite reciprocity in her partner. By giving up something of importance, it is expected that the other person should also give up something important to them for you. Not doing so becomes an insult because it seems like your sacrifice was devalued, and your partner feels guilty and remorseful that he cannot reciprocate to the same degree, i.e., drop everything that's important to him for you. It's also a situation that's beyond his control, really, because it involves a person with unbalanced priorities asking a well-adjusted person to become unbalanced.

Low self-esteem problems can lead a woman to think that a man will leave her if she doesn't make him and their relationship the center of the universe and that he doesn't continually reciprocate those feelings. Inside, these women don't feel they have qualities that are worth keeping.

Some couples are mutually lovey-dovey all the time, but most couples require a balance of independent priorities and relationship focus. Should men and women always be physically together and be lovey-dovey all the time? Is there something wrong with the relationship if a man and woman spend time away from each other to pursue hobbies and other interests? It really depends on how supportive each partner is. If, like Annie, they are haunted by the thought of communication loss, then that relationship is probably less than ideal.

BEING ON THE SAME PAGE

Being on the same page with your partner is important. In the early stages of your blooming relationship you are learning about him and vice versa. While the first few weeks may be devoted to romance, the consecutive months or years will tell you what's important to your partner and what kind of person he really is. If you get stuck inside the initial romance phase and refuse to move on and accept changes, then being in that relationship for the long term will be tough.

Is he looking for a real relationship, or something like friendship? Does he want to take it slow initially; perhaps so slow that there is no exclusivity? Discovering the answers to these questions could take a while, and rushing to know everything about him and his stand on your new relationship could be detrimental to his peace of mind. He hasn't decided yet, and like you, he is observing how you can handle the fact that he has other priorities that he needs to attend to.

For example, if he senses that you are going to make him give up some activities he loves, he could just balk at the thought of spending forever with you. One way to find out if he thinks this way is to observe how he handles your passions. Is he supportive of your priorities?

It's worthwhile to think about the first time you met him, what type of environment you met him in, and what event turned the tides for you and this guy. In short, what made him like you? If you sacrificed too much of your own priorities, there is a good chance that what you gave up was one of the primary things that attracted him to you.

ANNIE'S STORY (PART 2 OF 2)

When Annie walked into the coffee shop, the same one she used to work in, she had a gut feeling that this is the last time she will see her boyfriend. The past month has been a roller-coaster of emotions for them. She tried going with him to his volunteer tourist trips to show her support, but it always seemed like he was doing everything to keep them from spending time together. She became impatient and kept checking her watch, which bothered the guests and him.

She decided to stay quiet this time and just let him talk. He looked sad as he spoke and he didn't say much. Just this: "I walked into this coffee shop last summer and met the most wonderful, diligent woman in the world; a girl who was so gung-ho and eager to pay her college loans early. Who are you, and what did you do to her?"

ON THE FLIP SIDE: IS HE ASKING YOU TO CHOOSE?

What if the shoe was on the other foot? Would you feel guilty if a guy gave up many important things for you without your asking and then made you feel responsible for every single fight that happens? Standing your ground and fighting to keep doing what you do best is the most effective way to earn his respect early on. Tell him that you're good at what you do and he will have to live with that. If you are worried about drifting apart, share your concerns with him rationally and secure mutual commitments to make time for one another.

THE IMPORTANCE OF COMPROMISE

Compromise is the answer to a situation like this, and quality time is the vessel of this compromise. Give each other enough room to do other things. Don't ever belittle the worthwhile things that your partner does. Be interested, be involved; and most importantly, be involved in your own set of priorities. It's not about staying busy but cultivating who you really are that makes you attractive to another person.

Letting go of something important to you is not the solution, and it creates more problems. Men love passionate women, and this isn't always about sex. Women who are passionate about their goals, about improving themselves will be more successful with their relationships than those who are not passionate. Not having something as important as your own life's passion will make you a miserable partner, and that won't help your relationship. When he shows support, it means that your man wants you to succeed, so you have to put in your best effort to do so. Believe in your capacity to manage your time.

Know your place in his life, and make sure he knows his place in your life. Use your single lives as the time for doing all the things that you both will give up together to be able to build a family. This is a big thing in sustaining long-term relationships. It is important to think of the future and how much you both will enjoy a lifetime together if you don't stifle each other's inherent passions.

Some Tips for Creating the Right Ambiance for Quality Time Together

Be thoughtful; buy a small gift and prepare for the date like you're attending a prom. Bring a camera so you can document the place where you had dinner and for save it for a future scrapbook. Have a quick Valentine's weekend, even if it's not February yet. Better yet, make each date a Valentine's date. Travel together could make you feel like you're both leaving a place of stress and going to a place of relaxation. Leave the laptop at home and don't take work on the plane or road trip so you can spend that time talking.

Make your meet ups comforting and relaxed. After a busy week, connecting with your significant other physically and emotionally will soothe and take away the stress created by the long days of putting out fires in the work place, dealing with irrational people, and competing in the rat race.

Make it a habit to share a weekend together, or at the very least, an intimate lunch. Listen attentively to his opinions about things that are happening around you or at his workplace. Remind him to let go of the stress and at the same time, commit to making the date a special one by not bringing up any sensitive issues that you might fight over. Only give tough love when the situation demands it, and always practice caution and concern with his feelings.

Hug often while you talk and let each other's company prepare you for another hectic week ahead. Always keep your sense of humor when talking to your partner and laugh at his jokes.

Show your support by letting him know that you appreciate all that he does to improve himself. Be constructive in critiquing him and be emotionally available. He may already know that you are supportive, but hearing it from you will confirm it. Inspire him and let him be your inspiration.

THE DILEMMA OF CHOOSING zBETWEEN CAREER AND LOVE

The decision to give up something important in favor of love usually comes AFTER the courtship phase. This is definitely not something to get stressed out about before you even think about a person in the "husband and wife" sort of way. Having a career and making time for love is possible, but there are some things you have to give up somewhat when you decide to leave your single life and become a happily married couple. There are many factors which can affect your choice, and there is also the possibility that you won't have to choose at all.

Here's a story of a woman who didn't give up her interest even after marriage, and a description of the compromise.

Sandy and Raymond pursued their individual passions separately and managed to keep their relationship going despite the hardship of finding quality time together. For years it was ok, until they decided to have a baby and get married. Sandy knew she would have to give up her weekly mountain climbs to

> *have the baby, although Raymond never asked her to give it up. Instead of partaking in hikes, she decided to be a resource person for would-be hikers. Instead of abandoning her interest altogether, she now lectures on hiking several times a month and is completely satisfied with her choice.*

Sandy did not give up her passion of climbing, but she did embrace her new responsibilities with the same fervor. Limiting yourself to one aspect of the same interest, hobby, or even a career, can help in re-prioritization. You don't feel like you gave it up completely, and at the same time you are happy that your compromise effectively eliminated any guilt about pursuing your passions while in a committed relationship. There are people who know how to achieve a healthy life balance that allows them to live their lives to the fullest without sacrificing things that are important to them. Our priorities give us a sense of achievement in diverse but relevant ways that contribute to our self-esteem and self-worth. An individual could develop her whole identity based on what she does, what excites her, and what drives her to succeed.

Whenever you start to feel like you want to drop your priorities unnecessarily for the sake of love, remember that you have your whole single life to pursue your passions on your own before you absolutely need to make the choice between career, hobbies, and family.

You have needs and so does he. Do not force each other to choose love above all for now because being single and dating means doing everything you wish without really thinking of more pressing responsibilities. Does this drive home the point behind the term "settling down"?

Chapter 2: Are You Being Too Available?

if you think about it, wouldn't it seem logical that a man would appreciate that you're always available? Who wouldn't love someone who is completely devoted, giving, and willing to sacrifice their time? The truth is, when it comes to relationships, the more available you are, the less of a challenge you are.

Why do women rush in full throttle after a man shows the slightest interest? In this chapter you will discover what you can do to avoid being viewed as too available or too desperate. Acquiring self-worth is something that no one else can do for you, and to combat the imbalance of being too available, you'll need to start seeing yourself as a prize that men have to win.

HOW IT ALL STARTS

Being single means putting yourself out there to meet people. There are some single women, however, who overdo it. They get giddy with the slightest male attention and just grab rather than wait to be asked. Here's a dilemma of one girl who made herself too available for a guy and consequently drove him away.

> *It's been a few days since I met this amazing guy in a bar and he still hasn't called. What's stressing me out is that I think I know why. The more I think about it, the more I can see why he won't call at all. I probably sounded like a deranged woman calling him up, leaving a message on his voicemail and asking about his day. I think now would be a good time to admit*

> *that I was sort of drunk and too forward when I*
> *called. I doubt if he even remembers me, but after*
> *that great night together, how could he forget?*

Can men sense when you're desperate? Yes. Some can tell soon after he says hi to you and he notices the red hearts that form over your head. There's a big difference between making yourself desirable to a guy who's looking for love like you, and positioning yourself in such a way that wherever he turns, he sees you.

WE HAD SEX—WHAT NOW?

When after you had the best sex of your lives, he simply forgot about you, do not panic. Ask yourself if you really are into him or if he was really into you in the first place. Sometimes, people hook up for sex and sex only. While the ideal scenario would be for him to start a real relationship with you after the initial hook up, it doesn't always work out that way.

If he doesn't seem interested in anything else except for the hot night that you two shared, take it as a blow off and move on. Do not grovel, do not plead for him to look back and see you for who you really are beyond sex. He will look at you another way if there was something about you that he liked before the sex. If he does show a bit more interest, though, do not jump up and down in front of him and give him all your e-mail addresses, phone numbers, and street addresses. For example, "If you cannot reach me through these numbers, try my parent's house" is a big no-no.

When a girl who has slept together with a guy asks him, "Was it just sex to you?" there's a light bulb that goes off in his mind because he knows instantly that you want more from him that he may not be ready to give. It could be a relationship, a long-term affair, or simply another romp in the hay. The problem is that, when you ask him that question he may not be ready to answer or he doesn't want to answer at all because he doesn't want to hurt you or provoke a negative reaction. When a guy senses that you are making yourself too available for him, he might not want to go on another date with you. Men, like women, desire what they have to work for a bit to have.

Some guys feel the need to be polite. They come up with excuses not to see you again because they don't want to tell you the awful truth. If he did hook up with you only for sex, or even just small talk, you have to bear in mind that you still had him where you wanted him even for a while. This means that during that moment of attraction, you made him feel what it's like to be with you. Was he astounded by the way you can tackle an issue and make conversation? Was he swept away by your kisses? These are all signs of initial attraction. The trick is finding out how to keep him rapt and attentive.

WE DESIRE WHAT WE CANNOT HAVE

Do you remember your first prom dress? You went inside the shop to ask about it, try it on for a few minutes and walk around the shop wearing it, but you couldn't afford to buy it so you waded through the yellow pages to find potential employers. Every night you babysat for others and dreamed of that dress on the windowsill of your favorite shop. You thought about it so much that you could almost see yourself wearing it. Do you remember how you reacted when presented with the option of buying one of the cheaper dresses in your local flea market?

One of the cheaper, more readily available dresses is equally pretty, but somehow you don't want it. Settling for less than the one you really desire, or buying something that is less costly but equally available to anyone at anytime is not ad attractive of an option.

The Perception of Cheapness and Availability

We take for granted that things that are abundantly present at all times. When we get used to things that are constant, they become fixtures to us. A painting is just a painting until everyone wants to own it.

Even if you had sex already, if you have caught his attention in a way that you become unshakeable in his mind, he will pursue you and yearn for the time when you can be together again. You don't even have to do anything. Some women think that making themselves available for a guy all the time will make it easier for him to love her, or at the very least consider a long-term relationship with her, but it's the furthest from the truth.

There Is an Incubation Time for a New Romance

Men dislike being hounded immediately after they profess their liking, and in a similar manner, they dislike having to accommodate a relationship that has no value to them. This could come across as dense, but men need to find out for themselves why they like a girl. They need some time to reflect on why they went for the girl in the first place. Let his imagination do the work for you. Let him see you in his mind's eye and allow his brain to accentuate your best assets, your personality, and your beauty.

Not seeing you much during this time of romance incubation will increase the probability of arousing his curiosity even more. Turn the tables and see him in a new light. Won't you feel cornered if he stalked you right after your date? Wouldn't you freak out if he seems to be in all the places you go to?

Being "in his face" too much will decrease your value to him. He will be annoyed rather than flattered; irritated rather than seduced. A good guy will tell a girl directly "please give me time to miss you even for a second," while someone who doesn't feel inclined to be civil will simply close the door on you until he's ready to open his heart once again—usually for someone else.

You might have asked yourself the question, "Why make it difficult for him to get to me when I want him so much?" You might not see anything wrong with just calling him up daily, asking if he wants to go out, showing up at his favorite clubs, and even his local grocery store, but he will see that you want him so badly and cringe. Your forwardness will make him feel that you have lost some of your dignity. Not only is he no longer sure of his plans to get to know you more, he may even begin to question why he was into you in the first place.

SELF-WORTH AND SELF-CONFIDENCE

Before you begin dating, do a simple self-analysis to find out if you have some symptoms of the "too available" syndrome and stop yourself to prevent yourself from being embarrassed, dissed, and forgotten quickly. Ask yourself the following questions:

What is your love worth?

Are you in a panic?

Do you say, "I'll grab anyone who shows the faintest interest" quite often?

Do you say "YES" in your mind without being asked?

These questions seem funny, and sometimes a woman's panicked state and desperation could not be more obvious to men who deal with "too available" girls. If the girl doesn't put any value on herself, the man just might agree. Moreover, he may find that he doesn't want to date someone that he cannot yearn for sometimes. He also doesn't want to be the object of obsession. This kind of undivided attention and increasing visibility could betray the insecurity in the woman, and this is a big turn-off to men.

He won't feel challenged at all and will not exert effort to discover the best things about you because you volunteer every little thing every time you can. Besides, why would he put effort into taking you out on a date you when you're always right there anyway?

Men (and a lot of women) hate desperation in themselves and in others. Just getting the impression of desperation will make them run. For a long-term relationship to work, the initial courtship phase must be done right. Making him feel stifled by your constant presence could alert him to possible clinginess in the future. Worst of all, he might just think you're a crazy stalker type.

INCREASING YOUR SELF-ESTEEM WILL MAKE YOU MORE DESIRABLE TO MEN

Because desirable things are the most difficult to obtain, giving him a chance to miss you will increase your desirability and he will think of you more often.

Desperate women feel they simply must have a man—any man—in their lives to be complete. This kind of dependent attitude is too eager and servile, and ultimately drives would-be partners away.

Men and women react to each other based on the initial perceptions. Cultivating the thoughts that fuel desperation, such as "I will take what I can get. The first one to show affection, even" muddles your perceptions because you believe what you want to believe, see what you want to see, and hear what you want to hear. In your mind, maybe you are one hundred percent convinced that he wants you to always phone him, he has been trying to phone you all along but you were in the shower and that he wants to be with you but couldn't because someone is holding him hostage or something. Our minds justify another's actions because we have already set the initial belief in stone.

The most important thing is to not lose your objectivity when sizing up a new lover. Do his actions tell you that he doesn't really want a long-term relationship? Is he putting up with your constant bid for attention because he is too polite to really blow you off? Is he looking for a way to breathe again after your insistence that he see you daily?

Becoming panicked by possible rejection will contribute to a total lack of emotional control and your fears of being alone will feed the flame of insecurity.

Making yourself commonplace and free for anyone to pick on, pick up, and take home is a sign of weakness. You give out the vibe that just anyone can take your love and make it his own. The lack of self-esteem inspires pity rather than love.

Being desperation for attention makes you defensive and magnifies your lack of self-esteem to others. Correcting desperate thinking and behaviors will make you a more successful lover and would-be partner to a deserving guy.

Keep it Light

When you enter a new relationship, take it easy and make your life as normal as possible, but keep your intuition open for possible developments. When he contacts you, suppress your instinct to overreact and be willing to let him pursue you.

Rather than badgering him with questions about himself and trying to stuff years of knowing each other into the first week that you're together, give him time to reflect on your personality and why he should date you. In the meantime, you have to learn to keep your feet firmly planted on earth, even when your head is way up there among the clouds.

You simply can't make a relationship happen. It has to develop and grow like a bud that you nurture so it will blossom. Staring at the bud day in and day out will not make it bloom.

If he really isn't into you, don't feel sorry for yourself. Disappointed and sad, you learn the hard way that setting up unreasonable expectations based on your first date is partly fueled by your fear of losing the possibility of a new relationship. Remember that love, like a set of keys, will be found when you don't stress yourself out looking for it.

Men love attention, but not when it's coiled around their necks and their every reaction watched and evaluated. When it comes to attention, they will ask you when they feel like it. Give him the chance to ask you out, because requesting to date a woman he is smitten with is always a pleasure.

DEALING WITH PANIC

A single girl is acutely aware of her being single. The older she gets the more she feels like time is running out to find a suitable life mate. A typical single girl who is now ready for a relationship has spent quite a lot of time visualizing the rest of her life, and that usually includes being married, having kids, and being happy forever. The older she gets, the less likely this life she longs for will happen. She could also be afraid of getting old alone.

If you are in this situation, take a deep breath and gather your forces around you. Look yourself in the mirror and see the woman that you know you are. Any man will want you, and he will want you more if you make yourself the prized caviar rather than the commonplace catch of the day. Be visible, but suppress your preponderance to jump up and down when someone shows the slightest interest.

The greatest mystery of all is this: life starts when you discover ways to make your life fulfilling without needing anyone else to make it happen.

When you become content with yourself, you'll take things lightly, live life to the fullest, and you infuse your all of your actions with passion, and people will start to notice you. A man will see the partner that he wants to be with and you will have your pick of who you want to share your life with.

Playing the elusive card without overdoing it is the key to getting the happy married life you want. Stop being so available and people will know that you choose wisely, are not loose with your love, and that you value yourself enough for them to see you as a prize they have to win.

The Secret to Being the Girl All Men Want for a Long-Term Relationship

Self-confidence will turn him on more than an exposed cleavage or a nice leg show. Exuding self confidence in everything will get him excited to date you. It will make him curious on how you found peace with yourself. He will be confident that you are strong in character and will be able to deal with him and his own insecurities. Having a partner who is level-headed and comfortable with herself means there will be less drama, less hassle, less irrelevant fights, and less headaches overall.

Men can sense self-confidence as easily as they can detect a clingy, paranoid, and insecure girlfriend. Men will gravitate towards you, and like a priceless oil painting, they will bid for your attention more than you will bid for theirs. You don't have to be necessarily the most beautiful, smartest, or best-dressed woman in the crowd. A man who, like you, is looking for a long-term relationship will tune out the external appearance and feel out your personality. If you have all of these wondrous physical qualities, they will consider these a bonus, but these are the icing, not the cake.

People can tell what sort of a value you place on yourself. Your self-worth tells men that they should treat you well, be polite to you and give you time to decide whether you want to date them or not. Your well-balanced self-esteem is like a built-in mechanism that prevents a man from turning you into his doormat. Women who are selective and with reasonable standards can keep their head up in any situation. They are less likely to stalk a guy, much less beg men to like them by being too available.

The key to giving off that mysterious, elusive aura that get men crazy is knowing your place and being real with your limitations and strengths. You know your value and what you can offer. At the same time, you don't have any delusions about yourself.

You aren't desperate, and they know it. And, it makes them desperate to get to know you better. You become attractive in their eyes because they have a feeling that when they finally win you over, it will be pure bliss for them.

Chapter 3: Do Not Neglect Your Friends

One of the more stressful relationship issues is being able to balance platonic friendships with your new romantic relationship. As soon as a new relationship starts, some women leave their good friends behind in favor of a new beau.

A tight knit group of five girls had been together since childhood, all the way up through college, until one of the five had a boyfriend. Suddenly, the five became four. The girl left her friends to pursue her romance and never seemed to have any time for her friends.

You may have seen or even experienced this situation yourself in your dating life. Why did something like this happen? Similar to choosing love over work and school priorities, some women close the door on other people when they enter a relationship because they believe that choosing love over close friends is the ultimate sacrifice. Many times these same women become frustrated when their new man will not do the same. In some cases, some men make women choose between him and her friends— and the women agree! No man or woman should urge the exclusion of close friendships for the relationship. A healthy relationship has a balance between both.

During the initial phases of your relationship, you feel like you are living in a different world where everything's rosy and sane. As you embrace your new normal, you marvel at how wonderful life could be for someone who has found "the one." Every laughing moment turns hysterical, every dinner (even if it's just a sandwich) is absolutely delicious, and every date is sizzling hot. You don't care that you have been missing out on sleep; your head is in the clouds and you feel lustful, sexy, and desirable. This honeymoon period high can make you neglect a lot of friends and important priorities, like your job and personal interests. The uncomfortable truth that you won't admit even to yourself is that you feel no guilt, whatsoever, for this temporary memory lapse. Your feelings of bliss, for the moment, become top priority.

WHY YOU SHOULD NOT NEGLECT YOUR FRIENDS TO FOCUS ON YOUR NEW RELATIONSHIP

Maintaining close friendships is a long-term commitment. Even if you can't talk to your friends constantly like you used to before a relationship entered your life, keeping them abreast with what's happening in your life—and showing a continued interest in theirs—will make them feel like they're still a part of your life, and you're still a part of theirs.

Real friends help carry us in life. Of the many benefits they bring to our lives, they:

- **Do wonders for a suffering ego** during times when your relationship isn't stress free. When you're down, your real friends are there to pick you up and encourage you to keep going. Even if your boyfriend turns into your best friend, your other friends are still valuable resources for finding out what you're doing wrong and for affirming what you're doing right.

- **Keep us grounded** when we tend to live inside our minds too much. They share in the fun, they share in the worries, and they lend a helping hand when you desperately need comfort.

- **Bring out the best in our loyalty** when it is tested against a relationship. Standing up for your friends denotes faithfulness in friendship. While he could be closed-minded and resentful at first, he will soon appreciate the brand of loyalty that you have for other people as well as your admirable personal balance and independence.

A friend is someone that you know so well that you can predict what she will do next. She's the ultra-dependable shoulder to cry on, shopping companion, and loyal ally; but the next minute, she's carousing with her new boyfriend and leaving her long time friends in the dust. What happened?

First and foremost, these factors touch on her current self-esteem level, but they can also point to issues with her new boyfriend's preference and opinion of her friends, her friends' standards, and privacy issues. Let's take a closer look.

PROBLEM WITH PRIORITIES

As mentioned in chapter one, the priority trap could send someone who can't handle the pressure of balancing several things at a time spinning. When she ditches her friends for her new love, she may be so happy to have found love that she'll let nothing get in the way. She could also feel inferior about her boyfriend choice and doesn't want her friends to judge her harshly nor meddle with her decisions. Whatever the motivation, the reality is that choosing a unbalanced life usually gets in the way of love.

The good news is that there is also a chance that the behavior change is temporary. She is enjoying her new love life and she wants to test her relationship wings. Friends are very supportive and they won't mind initially, but if this goes on, they could feel rejected, dismayed, and neglected.

DID HE ASK HER TO?

In some new relationships, possessive boyfriend might not want to share his girlfriend with her own friends or his. This enforced exclusivity could be the guy's way of telling other people to back off from their relationship. The girl might resist but she wants to see how it works first, or she could be too insecure to fight for her friends' right to know about what's going on in her life.

In an ideal world, friends are supportive of new relation-ships and all members of the group immediately welcome new beaus to the group dynamics. Sadly, this is not always the case. There are irreconcilable differences among people stemming from conflicts in beliefs and philosophies, jealous misgivings, or simply insurmountable dislike.

One way to help mitigate those possibilities is to start everyone off on the right foot. It's important to look at the way they a new boyfriend is introduced to friends.

How to Introduce a New Boyfriend to a Discerning Group of Loyal Friends

People have several different ways of managing their friends and relationships. Some like to keep them apart, while some like to blend everyone together in a mixer. Considering that some friends will not relate to others very well and your boyfriend might not "dig" your friends and vice versa, the best introduction is one that is light and casual, yet planned ahead of time. If you keep communicating with your friends, they will know of your relationship updates anyway.

First, consider the environment when you introduce him. Will it be in a neutral environment like a coffee shop or a concert? Is there an issue that needs to be discussed among your friends? Are your friends in high spirits with no immediate cause for grief, stress, or tension?

Here are some ideal situations as well as situations to avoid when introducing your new boyfriend to the clan:

- **Shoot for a neutral environment.** A neutral environment keeps people civil, relaxed, and able to talk about pleasant things. A concert or a coffee shop introduction will also allow your friends to observe how the two of you look together and coordinate as a couple. Does he focus on you and your friends or does he keep glancing around to see if other women are in the vicinity? Your friends are your protector, and during introductions they'll act like your wingman to get a sense if he is the kind of guy who can make you happy or if he is putting on a lukewarm act.

A simple observation of how he handles you in the presence of company will tell a lot about how much he cares for you. If he takes you seriously, he will make an effort to downplay any behavior that could embarrass you, leave any manly "attitude" at home, and be on his most impressive behavior to make the initial introduction comfortable for everyone.

- **Avoid high-tension situations.** Introducing him to your friends while they are at war with some other entity or among themselves could be volatile. Seeing your friends this way could also be traumatic for your boyfriend. Make sure your friends are receptive to your boyfriend at the time of introduction, and vice versa. If this scenario cannot be avoided, it is best to tell him about the known issues so he won't be startled when two or more of your friends start making a scene or coming across as extremely negative.

- **Debrief sensitive topics beforehand.** If there are topics that simply must not be discussed when meeting for the first time, e.g., one of your friends just got divorced and your boyfriend just happens to be a divorce lawyer or a custody consultant, tell both your boyfriend and your friends ahead of time. Your troubled friend might not be up to discussing the issue and could clam up when prodded, and your boyfriend may not know how to approach the subject when presented with new information on the fly. After all, he wants to impress both you and your friends. Make it comfortable for everybody.

- **Make a payment plan.** Plan for who will pay for the food, accommodations, and other necessities ahead of time. If it isn't possible to coordinate with everyone, be prepared to pick up the tab yourself. Do not let your boyfriend shoulder the bill unexpectedly. If possible, split the bill with your friends to avoid making him pay anything, even if he offers. When a new boyfriend feels obligated to pay for everyone to make a good impression, it can build lasting resentment and set up your friends for unrealistic expectations about future outings. The best way to handle the bill is to pay your way as a couple.

THE INTRODUCTION AFTERMATH

After the initial introduction, a few things could happen. Your friends might not like your new boyfriend or think he's enough for you, or your boyfriend might not like them and begin to wonder how your relationship will work with them in the picture. Should this type of fallout arise, a girl needs to mediate between her friends and boyfriend—but not before she has heard everyone's opinion on the matter, separately.

If you're in the hot seat during your weekly or monthly meet-up with the girls is not a good place to bring your boyfriend, particularly if you brought him there to be your "ally" or to make a better second impression. So go it alone and despite strong feelings for your boyfriend, keep an open mind. Most friends have your best interests at heart.

WHAT IF MY FRIENDS DON'T LIKE HIM?

Have you heard this kind of statement or maybe even spoken this to one of your own friends before?

> *"Do you want my honest opinion? Your boyfriend is a know-it-all who will argue with anyone who disagrees about anything. You're the only one he's civil to, and that could change after marriage. Think, girl. Is this the kind of guy you want to end up with?"*

We trust our good friends because they have given us so much useful advice in the past and they know us well, but at what point is it okay to say, "I think you're wrong"? This dilemma usually pushes a single girl to "follow her heart," which is a nice way of saying she will soon ignore her friends who can't seem to understand that this is the guy who's making her happy, and it's her choice to stay with him.

Not all friends take this well. They will feel betrayed and confused about your decision because they care about you and won't understand why you can't share their viewpoint. They'll feel slightly resentful and will stay silent, waiting for any indication that your relationship is crumbling to hint or even say outright, "I told you so."

WHAT IF HE DOESN'T LIKE MY FRIENDS?

> *"Your friends are ... nice, but not really my speed. I kept looking at my watch and for the door. Let's not do that again."*

The first instinct is to jump to your friends' defense, but then you realize that his observation isn't completely baseless but you don't want it to impact your relationship. But still, how dare he insult your friends, and call them boring? Does this reflect on how he feels about you? You have associated with these people for years, and any insult to them is an insult to you. What's a girl to do?

MEDIATE TO ALLEVIATE CONFLICT

Ideally, you can mediate between your friends and boyfriend, either together by creating more opportunities for them to get along, or you can talk to them separately to explain why you cannot give up one for the other. There may be many factors why each camp feels animosity towards the other and they could be related directly to you, but several factors out of your control like basic personality differences may come into play.

No matter how complex the factors driving the disconnect between your boyfriend and your friends, try these steps:

- **Group intervention.** You can try to set up a conversation between them to air all ill feelings out. They just might discover how trivial they're being, and how stressed out you are from being put in the middle of all the animosity. Make them understand that they are both important to you in your life and therefore a compromise must be reached.

- **Agree to disagree.** When all else fails, you can request a civil compromise. Let you friends know that you appreciate their insight and advice, but that you want to try to make a relationship happen with your boyfriend because he makes you feel good to be with. True friends will at least be supportive of that fact. Then tell your boyfriend that you respect his feelings but that your friends have been with you through thick and thin, and that they are necessary to your happiness. Any man worth his salt will be supportive of that, even if he doesn't like your friends. When you get both parties to agree to disagree, they can choose to be civil with one another when you meet up together, or in extreme cases you can simply split your time and be with them on different occasions.

IS A "CHOICE" NECESSARY?

"My boyfriend, best friend, and me all belong to the same circle. Everyone used to get along but now, they can't stand to be in the same place together. We never talk about it. I go out with each of them separately and dread the time when I will have to choose between them."

You may not have to choose between your boyfriend and your friends. You can spend Fridays with your boyfriend and Saturdays with other friends. If you start getting sick of this, you can re-evaluate your options. If forced to make a stand, you can simply deliver your ultimatum to both camps and be firm about it.

Keep in mind that jealousy might be present through this whole ordeal on both sides. Could they be afraid of losing you? Once you have convinced both your boyfriend and your friends that they aren't losing you, and that in time they can learn to get along, you may see changes.

TRUST YOUR GUT FEELINGS

When in love, you may be living in a fantasy world and might not be able see what you would otherwise if you weren't so smitten. Could your friends be right? Believe in your boyfriend because he could just become your partner someday, but keep your eyes open for signs that your friends are right all along. Maybe he isn't right for you.

Here's a way of finding out the real deal about the conflict, if there is one. Single out your most trusted, objective friend in the group and have a long heart-to-heart talk with her. Have a mini-bitch session and just let loose. It's easier to deal with one friend who really knows you, than a mob of turbulent emotions that can erupt when you're talking to all of your friends at once.

STAND YOUR GROUND

Strength comes when you persist. Your friends may not realize that you can handle a guy like that, and so they become overprotective. Showing them that you are determined to make it work with your new beau could radically change your friends' perception of you and shut them up about the issue once and for all.

Tell your friends what you like about him, and vice versa, in an objective manner. Being emotional during a crisis like this could tear you apart and lead you to say things that you don't mean. It's possible that your new boyfriend is nervous about impressing your friends, says the wrong things, and rubs everyone the wrong way. Nonetheless, time is an ally in this situation, particularly when all you can seem to do is divide your time and wait it out.

RISKING IT

When you have tried mediating and both parties still won't see the light, you can risk it and let them talk without you. There's a big chance that your presence is making them uncomfortable saying what they really want to say to each other. You trust your friends, you trust your boyfriend, and you trust yourself not to overdo it (or overreact!). You have to make it clear to them that the issue really bothers you, makes you feel helpless, and causes so much guilt that you can barely function anymore.

Don't burn bridges among your friends, and don't mediate in a way that it's unclear whether one party wants to compromise with the other. Give each the benefit of the doubt and always think that they have your best interests at heart.

HE COULD APPRECIATE YOUR TIME WITH YOUR FRIENDS

If you decide to keep your love life and your other friend-ships separate, your boyfriend might like it! Unless he is paranoid, delusional, or afflicted with a serious inferiority complex, your time off from him could be a welcome respite. He knows you love your friends and being without you for a while could be bearable to him because he knows you're with people you love and who love you back.

When out with your friends, make the time to update them about yourself, not just in the context of your relationship, but you alone. What have you been up to? How's work? Sometimes, our friends get sick of hearing how happy we are that we have new boyfriends and would rather hear something neutral.

Continue to be a good friend. Do not forget friends' birthdays and anniversaries. Make sure you still remember their children's names. If you can't do it in person, make sure to send a thoughtful gift that will remind your friend that you keep her or him in mind at all times.

MOMENT OF WEAKNESS

If you have decided to give in and risk losing your friends just so you and your boyfriend can have all the time in the world, is it just fair to make him give up his friends too? The answer is no. You made your own choice to leave others behind, but forcing him to do the same for the sake of fairness is both unjust and upsetting.

When handling relationships, particularly in scenarios in which you cannot do anything about a certain issue, the key is to keep a level head. Trusting your judgment will also be helpful when the going gets tougher. Keep the hope alive that they will soon see the light and make peace with each other. No, you can't just "forget'" about your boyfriend because your friends said so, and vice versa. Trust that time is on your side and that it will heal the rifts that happen. Don't burn permanent bridges for the sake of what may be a temporary romance, but persist for as long as it takes for everyone to be friends with each other, even if it takes forever.

It's a "damned if you do, damned if you don't" situation, but your best chance of getting peace of mind is to continue on with your relationship while keeping your skeptical friends at bay. They may not realize that you are staying with your man even if they don't like him because you see something in him that they don't. Your devotion will convince them that there must be something good in him after all.

BOND THROUGH ACTIVITIES YOU CAN ALL DO TOGETHER

One way to heal rifts between friends and boyfriends is to plan bonding activities that are planned cleverly to center around activities all of you enjoy. Keep the public displays of affection minimal and focus on fun. You might try hosting a:

- **Cookout**. Form a team and start a cook-off contest. Everyone will contribute to a delicious win (or not so delicious, depending on team skills!) that will be a lot of fun. It's a great way to foster teamwork in action.

- **Picnics**. A potluck beach party is great for bonding. Bring a dish to enjoy, a volleyball net and ball, and challenge each other to a game. Like a cook-off, teamwork encourages camaraderie and engaging in sports is a great way to re-introduce your boyfriend to your friends.

- **Fishing trip.** With everyone working together to catch lunch, things are bound to be festive and light. Your friends might just realize that your beau is a great catch.

Do not be afraid to let your boyfriend mingle with your friends. A pleasant and neutral environment is the best venue for everyone to feel comfortable enough to get to know each other. Even the haughtiest of friends can warm up to your boyfriend so long as everything is kept light and fun.

Chapter 4: The Role of Real Friends and How to Spot the Paparazzi Pals

there are real friends who only want the best for your relationship, and there are spectator friends who wait for relationships to fail for their entertainment.

Distinguishing between the two can play a big role in the success of your relationship with a would-be partner.

We learned about how our friends play a big role in our lives in Chapter 3. Everyone exists in an ecosystem built around friendships and relationships. You might have noticed how you feel tension even when it's a close friend who's having relationship trouble. This empathy is normal among friends and we are blessed to have them in our lives.

Yes, friendship is very important in a relationship, but only if real friends are involved. These people help keep us grounded and be true to ourselves. However, when dealing with relationships, there can be clues that tell us when good friends turn bad.

The paparazzi have always been regarded as a bane of every celebrity's private life. They keep coming at the celebrities who want nothing more than a quiet day at the park. They hog your free time and watch like a hawk as your marriage falls apart, snapping photos along the way.

Real friends, on the other hand, help us in our relationships. Understanding their positive impact will make us more aware of mere paparazzi pals who only want to be spectators in our lives, and who couldn't care less if we end up being happy or miserable; just as long as they have something to talk about.

THE PROPER WAY OF LOOKING FOR RELATIONSHIP SUPPORT FROM YOUR FRIENDS

Emotional isolation from friends in romance is just as bad as putting your relationship on the front page of a newspaper. Not everyone will give you great relationship advice, but those few gems you call your *real* friends are those who:

- how good values and point of views regarding commitment

- Exude a positive aura and dishes out constructive criticism

- Don't meddle unless asked

- Are not pushy and nosy

- Respect your privacy

Relationship support is one pillar of a good union, and at the start of a new romantic relationship comes in the form of counseling, forums, or one-on-one conversations. Make a list of the friends who have always shown the above traits as well as those individuals and couples you admire. Being positive can be the key to a lasting relationship, and your relationship will benefit greatly from the experiences of people in your life that have been married or together for a long time (and feel lucky to be with the same person). These couples act as emotional resources for you and your new boyfriend. Ask them to share their relationship secrets that have worked for them throughout the years.

There are also those real friends who are single and who can talk to you about you. These are your best friends who know you inside and out, and will always be there for you when you need them. These people can be your relationship mentors; they may not see all sides of your relationship, but they will always empathize when needed and stay quiet about every detail you share with them. Most of all, they will encourage you to commit, be romantic, be happy, and be responsible.

These people give tough love, and their advice could be difficult to swallow. However, having them around is comforting because they have your best interests at heart. They may say the uncomfortable truth and be frank about everything, but we know them to be true, so we trust what they say.

On the other hand, when your circle of friends includes individuals who have been disillusioned with love and you feel like you and your partner are struggling to stay afloat in a sea of broken individuals and their failed relationships, you might start to see your relationship in an unnecessarily negative light. There are hundreds of communities that aim to encourage starting couples, and your goal should be to make friends with those who are positive about relationship issues and who won't weigh you down with never-ending talks of divorce, separation, messy breakups, or relationships that will never work.

ENTER THE PAPARAZZI PALS!

These kinds of "friends" are not hard to spot. They are the ones who keep talking about how your new boyfriend is so wrong for you as soon as they meet him for the first time. The weird thing is that even if they are bashing him, they somehow continue to eat up your description of how your date went and how wonderful he is to you.

They simply meddle, meddle, and meddle some more with your relationships, sometimes to the point of causing irreparable damage to your union with your boyfriends. Once you give these pals a reason to intrude, they will come at you with full force.

You have a new relationship and you are excited to tell all your friends. Some friends are nosier than others but you don't care. You start spewing the details of how you and the guy met and fell in love and the current status of your relationship. As soon as you let him meet your group, several people have befriended him and want to know his version of how the two of you hooked up. Some even went as far as ask for his number. You don't feel threatened and you even feel flattered. After all, they are all your friends and they want the best for you, right?

There's a real danger in letting your new beau inside your circle too soon after you start dating. Our real friends are there to make him feel welcome, but some others like the paparazzi pals may see what you saw in him and make him feel "more welcome" than others. Common friends are fun, but there are privacy issues that erupt between you and your boyfriend when everyone wants a piece of your relationship.

In an ideal world, everyone would respect each other's relationship, and not nose around in a friend's current affairs just to have something to talk about with others. When you hear of friend or boyfriend stealing, it usually involves allowing paparazzi pals a free ticket into their private lives in name of apparent camaraderie. While it's natural to give your friends the benefit of the doubt freely, it's in your best interest to distinguish between a real friend and a paparazzi friend.

RANT: MY RELATIONSHIP IS NOT A SOCIAL EXPERIMENT IN A FISHBOWL

Sharing your relationship troubles with common friends freely can make your boyfriend feel like a fish in an aquarium or a loser in a televised social experiment. Feeling like he has been under the microscope for so long, he wants out.

The pressure of everyone knowing about your love life is so great and the stories about you become so convoluted that even you believe them. If you followed what tabloids say about celebrity breakups, you will realize just how too much media exposure can help kill a relationship. Friend feed, or sharing a blow-by-blow account of what's happening in your relationship can lead to serious issues. Remember that there's a thin line between sharing a part of what's happening and being an all-out tattle-tale. Do not turn your relationship into a media circus.

Asking for your friends' take on every single detail of your relationship could alert him to the fact that you cannot make your own decisions.

Your boyfriend might understand that you have a few friends who have your ear, but a whole community of advisors called on for every decision you make is a group-sponsored way of living life. Some guys are very private, and don't like explaining all of his actions to a girl, much less to everyone in her circle. He would rather see you solve your relationship problems on your own before you go around conducting a survey, especially one that involves the private union you share.

The key to balancing your private and public aspects of your relationships is to delineate which issues to keep private and which ones to dish out on everyone's plate. It also helps if you can differentiate who your true friends are and which ones are only eaten up with envy only covered by a smile. While boyfriend or friend stealing smacks of emotional immaturity and irrationality, it happens more often than we'd like to admit.

THE PROFILE OF A BOYFRIEND STEALER

Here's an interesting excerpt from a boyfriendstealer.com that zeroes in on how a boyfriend stealer thinks about the value of your boyfriend:

> *"They have generally been selected with some care and attention to detail. Sort of like a handbag that you wouldn't look at twice before you've seen it dangling from the shoulder of your very trendy friend. Or a pair of second-hand jeans that could only get "that look" through many washes and wears by some diligent fashionista."*

Could there be someone within your group of friends who has started seeing your boyfriend in a different light as you talk daily about how GREAT he is in bed? It's the carrot that dangles in front of the horse. The horse might not get to it at all, but it will definitely try its best. While you can seem to trust all your friends and most of them have only good intentions, talking all the time about how awesome your relationship is will make other people envy you. At the very least, your incessant storytelling could make others feel like you're bragging to them.

But don't be obvious about your distrust because it can cause others to see you as paranoid. However, if you have that nagging gut feeling that one of your friends may be checking your week-old relationship out to see if she can butt in whenever she wants, be cautious, and heed these tactics to insulate your relationship against a potential boyfriend stealer from within your own circle of friends:

- **Build a backbone before introducing him to your circle.** Allow enough time alone with you and your new beau to solidify the beginning stages of a relationship before you introduce him to your friends. Introducing him too early could send the signal to boyfriend stealers friends that your union with him is not serious yet and is therefore fair game.

- **No digits; no exceptions.** Never let him give his phone numbers or e-mails to your friends, particularly to those who are asking for it if you and your boyfriend aren't already in a more solidified relationship.

- **Heed selective counsel.** If you have relationship trouble, talk only to your real friends about it. If he feels the need to talk to one of your friends about you, tell him who you trust most among your pals so he will know who to approach.

- **Say no to solo friend dates.** Never encourage him to go out drinking with your girl pals without you. Also, watch out for those ask him out for "friendly" dates alone—that crosses the line and those "friends" should be put on your "watch closely" list.

There's a thin line between trust and distrust, so you have to be very careful when walking that tight rope. Envy is a capital sin, and when you have a relationship that other people covet, you have to be on your toes.

The problem is that you don't know what some of your pals are capable of doing. You think you do, but you really don't. Those who have always harbored a secret envy for things you have or have achieved may just see your happiness in a new relationship as the straw that broke the camel's back. You already own an abundance of everything, and why don't they help themselves to a piece of your pie?

Trust Yourself and Your Partner to Make Your Relationship Thrive

These paparazzi pals may gab all they want about you, your boyfriend, or your relationship, but it will all fall on deaf ears if you and your boyfriend have a solid regard for one another. Trust him to make the best decisions and keep your head up. Regardless of what anyone says, he was attracted to you for a reason and you must believe that your relationship will thrive despite the fair-weather friends who threaten to intercede.

By cultivating the ability to objectively observe paparazzi and boyfriend-stealing "friends," you'll know who you're dealing with and can distance yourself and your relationship out of harm's way.

Stick by those friends who have proven time and time again that they are trustworthy. When those you have deemed as paparazzi pals ask for the "juicy details," resist the urge to dish the dirt and keep your explanations simple and vague.

You might also want to analyze why you feel compelled to tell people about how happy you are. If your motives include making people envy you, you might have serious self-esteem issues that you haven't dealt with yet.

Chapter 5: Stop Putting Him on a Pedestal

before you go too far, too fast in a relationship, it's important to consider how too-high expectations are formed and why putting him on a pedestal leads to heart-break, or at the very least, misunderstanding. If you're honest with yourself about who he is—both his strengths and limitations—you'll avoid suffering from disillusion-ment later on.

BUILDING THE PEDESTAL

In the beginning of a relationship, it's all about hearts, giggles, and roses. Some call it the days of loving; those silly days when you could just stare at each other's eyes and exchange mushy love notes and SMS messages all day. You're both so high on each other and nothing at all can keep you apart. This period lasts for three to six months and during this time you're so in love that you're spellbound by even his most mundane quirks. You'll find yourself repeating things he said to you to your friends, and you'll daydream all day about your previous dates, and how his every smile seemed to melt you.

This phase goes on for a while before your friends, family members, and even your boss may ask you: "Do you really know this guy well enough to start talking about forever with him?"

It is during this relationship stage that we build pedestals—elevated structures that represent how well we value someone we are head-over-heels in love with. While this sounds positive, elevating someone we just met to hero status could be detrimental to a single girl's psychological health. When you place a man on a pedestal, you don't know what he does, because you are worshipping him from below. You might not see everything from your vantage point and if the pedestal is high enough, you might not even trust the judgment of other people who could be seeing him from a more level angle.

When we start dating, we have about what qualities our boyfriends should possess. We tend to define our standards in terms of verifiable factors, such as educational background, financial status, and relationship track record. These standards comprise the bricks and mortar e that we use to build our pedestal.

Here are a few examples of pedestal-building thoughts:

- *He graduated from a top university so he must be smarter than the other guys I've met in the past. This also means he makes good decisions, is thorough with his actions, and is determined to succeed. He aced his SATs so he must be a diligent hard worker and a really studious guy who never had time for parties.*

- *He is spotless in appearance. This means he must be very conscientious with his hygiene. It's wonderful that he's like this. I wouldn't want a slob!*

- *He has donated more to charity than he uses to live each day. He must be very generous and giving to the less fortunate. I'd love a guy who gives without asking for anything back.*

- *He's a home-to-office, office-to-home kind of guy. He doesn't go drinking much and he likes the home life. He must be family oriented, and would love to simply lounge around the house with me when he's not working. He will be a wonderful father.*

- *He's loaded! He will take care of me and my needs for sure! I will not have to work. I might even be able to hire maids and what-not!*

The beginning of a relationship is the time for illusions. You take everything at face value, and give him the benefit of the doubt at every turn. The initial months after you two meet will also establish the pace and the future possibilities of your relationship. Will it be successful? It depends on how you start it.

One thing's for sure: building a pedestal for him to sit on while you bustle to worship and fawn over him is not the best way to start a lasting relationship. In the first place, he might not want to encourage your thinking that he is infallible. He is far from perfect and he knows it. At the very least, it will make him uncomfortable.

There are certain guys, however, who enjoy being on that pedestal that you so conveniently propped up for him. He will sit there and preen when you're looking on, and still be human, with a myriad of limitations and weaknesses when you're looking elsewhere. A man cannot be faulted for encouraging your illusion. It is your doing. He is your hero and is needed to act out the role. Just understand that it can set you up for disappointment later when your illusions go head to head with reality.

DOES HE REMIND YOU OF SOMEONE?

Could his facial features, body proportions, way of walking and talking, accent, or job remind you of a relative, even someone who passed away? A lot of women get attracted to men who have an uncanny resemblance to a loved one.

Subconsciously, women find similar traits in men they have relationships with. Do you know someone who only dates guys who have a certain way of talking, body proportion, or gait? It may have something to do with the quality of the men she has been exposed to and who have been around during her formative years. Filling her life with past "hero" replicas contributes to the delusion that these men all possess a specific set of good qualities and invincibility, which may not be true. She's built the pedestal, strengthened it and now, she needs a person to place there... her new boyfriend.

YOUR HERO

Becoming the leader of your boyfriend's own one-woman cult is willingly setting yourself up to be deceived. He no longer has to enforce his will on you. You will adore him no matter what and to you he can do no wrong, even in the face of contrary evidence.

Once your hero gauges the extent of your devotion, he may realize that he could just as easily fool you into thinking that he's not doing anything wrong. Heroes don't cheat. Heroes don't lie. Heroes like your straight laced dad are always devoted to one woman and one woman alone. But your hero and the hero you are imagining may not be the same person.

HIS TRUE COLORS

We all hide our hang ups and deep-seated issues at the onset of any relationship. After all, we're trying to impress another by putting our best qualities first. You can't force a guy to show his true colors when he's too busy impressing you, feeding your fantasy, and fanning your hero worship, But understand that less desirable insecurities and attitudes could be just below the surface. It's safe to assume that there will be something you're not initially seeing, like a weakness, limitation, bad attitude, or at worst, a dirty little secret.

Like anything else that's hidden, it's only a matter of time before it rises to the surface. If you are blinded with love, though, and he's still on the pedestal you built for him, you probably won't notice at first. When or how a person shows that he is undeserving of your pedestal depends on how far gone you are in terms of thinking of him in the "hero" sense. But remember, he is human.

Like you, he will move out from the romance phase, and perhaps spend time getting to know you more deeply, dealing with who you really are without the benefit of rose-colored glasses. His way of observing you could be different, but the objective is the same. He'll discover your strengths and weaknesses and decide whether he can live with these personal traits in a partner. The problems arise when you don't do the same to him.

If you communicate that your belief is that he is someone who has few weaknesses, he might feel pressured to keep that belief alive.

Meanwhile, he could really want you to see him as he really is: a human being who isn't perfect. There are a lot of men who dislike the pedestal; what it is made of, and what it represents. Men who notice how high your expectations are could just balk at the thought of spending forever with you because it's too much work for them.

For the really devious ones, however, you are ego fodder. They will string you along, sit comfortably on the nicely padded pedestal, and enjoy the adoration. Usually, these are the men who are keen on keeping you deluded, have no respect for your self-esteem, and won't care if your servile attitude could lead to trauma on your part when they tire of you and move on to someone else—and they will when they don't feel like playing the game anymore.

HOW TO TAKE HIM OFF THE PEDESTAL AND SEE HIM AS HE IS

After that first couple of weeks or months when things are absolutely amazing, lusty, and fulfilling, a girl must do what she has to do: observe, research, and decide if he is truly a good partner. Love and sex plague our initial romance phase and cloud the mind, but with the waning of lust, you can think objectively.

Observe some inconsistencies in behavior; research a few things from his other relationships (by simply asking about it or learning his pattern in relationships from other sources), and decide if you can live with his weaknesses. If not, it's time to move on.

Here are three steps that will help you move from pedestal building to viewing him on more equal ground:

1. **Reverse the hazy notions you had of him during the beginning of the relationship.** Did we gloss over the dark stuff and refuse to acknowledge some glaring bad attitudes because we were so happy? Easing off our self-made blind spots can be very tricky, but it's easy enough to see the things we failed to see then if we keep our minds open.

2. **Accept human traits of fallibility.** The hero image that you worship becomes attached to this guy because of the innate fear of falling for someone who is less than what we want. Uncovering the layers of illusions we set up starts with the first fallibility that appears, and although it can be a tough transition to accept his imperfections, they are part of who he really is.

3. **Cherish his uniqueness.** You already know that he is different from most of the men you met before, and right now, the goal is to discover just how unique he is. Does he let his insecurities show by being jealous like the other guys, or does he have a unique way of dealing with jealousy? How good is he at handling your drama? Does he even bother to hear you out?

Love takes on another form after the honeymoon phase. Gone will be the intense love that sent you to heights of passion, and in its place a love that focuses on the real emerges. Your goal is to love the person without the pedestal, on a level which you can relate to him as a real living person who may or may have the qualities you desire in a partner.

STRENGTHS AND WEAKNESSES

Discovering the other person's strengths will help keep the love alive between you. They could be observed in many ways, including during day-to-day activities such as picking up laundry or doing errands. If he's methodical and systematic, you might value that. His skills in money management could be another strength that you will adore about him. The important thing to consider when looking at a person's good traits is whether you can learn from them or not. If his approach to an issue or situation inspires you in a way that you want to emulate it, then consider it good.

On the other hand, weaknesses are the qualities in a person that you'd rather not see. Dealing with your weaknesses is difficult enough, and so seeing another person's weakness could be a real challenge. Nonetheless, there is no other way to start accepting a person's true self but to square your shoulders and accept it with an open mind, still keeping in mind how his weaknesses could affect you as an individual and the future of your relationship. You could wince or whine about his weaknesses, and sometimes successful compromises can be reached. However, it is a fact that you can only ask for compromise on some of his weaknesses; those that you really cannot live with.

CAN YOU LIVE WITH HIM WITHOUT THE PEDESTAL?

So, he's human. He makes mistakes, he may or may not apologize for them and sometimes he might even delude you or himself about his mistakes and limitations. However, through the struggle of getting to know him, he will appreciate your efforts at getting to know who he really is and perhaps even caring enough for him to love him *despite* his many weaknesses.

One of the best ways of finding out what he's all about is to show him around your world and see how he reacts to every kind of situation that you deal with on a daily basis. Evaluating how he acts and adjusts to a variety of environments is the best way to get to know your boyfriend. One warning: do not create scenarios to put him on the spot. With this, I mean follow the golden rule. If you don't want being thrown in a situation that's beyond your control, you should not go out of your way to do it to your beau.

Here are some examples of daily situations that could help you determine his true character. Be aware that a lot of these scenarios are rife with stress and tension, whether imposed by you or external factors.

- **Family gatherings.** Events that take on the aura of a Brady Bunch episode will show you how he is when around people. Weddings and funerals, in particular, could show you how he can deal with extremes of emotion in you or other family members, specifically happiness and grief. Family traditions will bring out the worst and the best in people. There could be one tradition that he likes and so he goes along with it, or there could be one particular tradition that he really abhors, and lets everyone see his disapproval. There is no mistaking it, everyone wants to get to know him better and tries to make him feel welcome. How does he feel about being the main participant of a parlor game? How about some games wherein a couple is required to participate; does he feel embarrassed at showing his affection for you to your whole family?

- **Going on a trip together.** Traveling to a new location is tiring, stressful, and trying, at best. Observe how he acts when things don't go as planned, when flights get delayed, or when a tour guide misses a critical intersection and you end up lost in a wilderness somewhere deep in the Amazon. Does his stress add to the tension of the people around him? Does he shout and spout expletives at no one in particular? Could he be blaming everyone but himself?

- **When you break his stuff.** Accidents happen. You know it; he knows it. So, what happens when you accidentally spill coffee on his designer jeans or when you mess around with his computer and accidentally delete a saved file containing work he labored over for weeks?

WHY YOU CANNOT BREAK UP WITH YOUR EX

Years or months after a relationship, do you find yourself still yearning for a guy you split with in the past? Do you measure each guy you meet according to a benchmark which weirdly resembles your ex?

This is one rule of moving on that you should always remember: do not put your past relationship or notions of your ex on a pedestal.

You are grieving, sure, but this doesn't mean you have to convince yourself that "you will never find someone as wonderful as your ex-boyfriend." Infatuation or hero worship can easily be mistaken as true love. That fact that you never saw anything wrong with the guy means you did not look closely enough. He is neither a superhero nor a demigod. He has his weaknesses that you were never exposed to or never accepted as even existing. Longing for him means you miss his company, which is normal. However, making him your idol or epitome of the perfect guy is disastrous to your future love life.

Chapter 6: Are You Changing Yourself To Please Him?

*Y*ou *just met an amazing guy at a party and did your best to impress him. He asked for your number from a common friend. Chances are, he's into you, and you are stoked! "Now," you think, "What can I do to become the perfect girlfriend for this amazing guy?"*

While you can put your best qualities and attributes forward, what pushes a girl to give up her sense of self to please her boyfriend? There are men who are worth the compromise, and will appreciate the effort, but there are those who won't even notice. And, of course, there is always the possibility that you are changing for him even when not asked. It can be difficult to determine whether when is change good and when it causes imbalance in a relationship. How do you know when to compromise and when to let go?

YOUR QUEST TO BE THE "PERFECT GIRLFRIEND"

You might have heard from others how well their relationships are going. You might search for tips on how to please your guy and give him what he wants. Some of these things require you to tweak a lot of the aspects of your personality, but you do it in the name of love.

"In the name of L.O.V.E.!" you tell yourself, as you scramble to overhaul your personality to fit his. Let's say you have always been the geeky sort (read: book in hand, coffee break while reading time, poetry writing, and book writing), but your new boyfriend is someone who socializes a lot because of his job in sales. You then give your "old life" an overhaul and hope it doesn't come back to haunt you. The trouble is, you don't know when you are going to break from all the stress of going out a few times a week, shopping for new things (because people have already seen you in all of the outfits you have in your closet!), and being at his side at all his sales functions.

A few months of this and you're exhausted. There are times when you simply want to curl up in a couch with a good book. You gasp as you realize that it's your "old life" calling you back, and you shudder at what he would think. You even may become resentful because you're not being who you are.

Question one: Did he like you for who you are? Does he even want you to change your lifestyle for him?

One day, you just break down and tell him that you can't do it anymore. Over coffee one morning, he looks at the dark circles beneath your eyes and says, "Why sweetie, I thought you enjoyed these things more than I did. I was surprised, even, that you turned out to be a social butterfly, when all along I though that you were Jessica's quiet friend."

You see, there are men who ask you out because they liked an aspect of you that is special and unique. In this case, he could have been looking for someone who is a bit more introverted and someone he can spend quiet weekends with. The thing is, you took it upon yourself to change for him because you thought he wouldn't like the "real you."

Question two: Do you think the "real you" is not good enough for him? Do you have a self-acceptance problem that impacts your relationships?

Each of us has something to offer a relationship, and most times, others see that before we see it in ourselves. Someone who is seriously into you will accept you as you are, and even more than that. In fact, he could have wanted someone exactly like you. Now, why don't you accept yourself more when he obviously does?

Are you changing yourself in the hopes that he will stay forever? Do you "adapt" to his needs? Volunteering to be everything to him is not the way to start a healthy long-term relationship. Sooner or later you will realize that you cannot be everything to him, and this will cause undue stress. Take it easy, relax, and bask in the comfort of a relationship built on a common ground that only you two know about.

Could he be a closet silent type too? Is he a hidden romantic or a poet who is thrust into a world of sales letters and socializing daily? Whatever qualities in you that attracted him are special aspects that you show, so why change them?

Lesson From "The Runaway Bride"

If you remember the Julia Roberts movie entitled "Runaway Bride," you'll get the drift about what can happen when you make the mistake of losing your identity in a relationship. Not knowing who you really are and depending on your relationship to find your identity for you will always result in unresolved issues that can lead to commitment problems. In the movie, Julia Roberts plays a woman who jumps in and out of relationships because she doesn't know who she is. She took a break from carrying all the emotional baggage and found herself before she offered marriage to a guy she truly liked.

Sometimes self-esteem, self-worth, and self-realization often get labeled as "no big deal." But in determining relationship quality, it is a huge deal. Finding out what you want for yourself and the things you like to do, setting appropriate goals you would like to achieve, and understanding your personal intentions, inner nature, and true calling is key to realizing what you can offer in a relationship.

His strengths and your strengths will push the relationship far enough to last the rest of your lives, while your limitations can be looked upon as a project in the works for both of you. Your mutual cooperation to deal with each others' limitations will spell the difference between a nasty breakup and a sustainable relationship.

SHOULD YOU LOSE YOUR IDENTITY TO "SAVE" A RELATIONSHIP?

If you think that the "ultimate sacrifice" of giving up the ideals, activities, and pleasures that make you the way you are will be the key to a lasting relationship, you are mistaken. It is the things that you do each day for yourself and for your relationship that will determine your happiness and satisfaction, as well as that of your partner. Giving to yourself and to him is the best way to make a relationship prosper, but until your self-esteem is where it should be, the "giving to self" often becomes sacrificed.

RELATIONSHIP BURNOUT

"How much longer can I keep this up?" is the question that starts the process of a breakup. Whether you say it out loud when you're alone or to a good and trusted friend, there are major issues in your current relationship. Not dealing with them appropriately will inevitably cause it to end.

The extension of infatuation with relationship or a guy can sometimes be heady, and you love the no-sleep nights and dreamy waking hours, but there will come a time when you will have to settle for "ordinary days." These are the days that follow the honeymoon period of a relationship. When it is over you will need to get in touch with the all of the priorities and activities that that you used to do on your own before your new relationship began.

During the lull that follows your dreamy state, you will realize that our overly hyped mind cannot maintain a continuous love overdrive. It needs to rest, and during this period you will need to regroup emotionally to be able to think clearly about how the relationship might progress in the future. You might even show some symptoms of a relationship burnout. You're not doodling his name on a sketchpad or an organizer page anymore; you realize that he has annoying habits that exasperate you at times, and after a hard day at work, you're surprised that all you want is to sleep.

Usually, after three to six months of being together, the issues will show. This is the time when the stuff you did to put your best foot forward will end. If you have been deluding yourself that your relationship is absolutely flawless during your honeymoon, then you might have a hard time surviving the months or years that will follow.

At the onset of any relationship, be real, stay real as the relationship moves on from the honeymoon period, and put your real foot forward. He will appreciate it in the long run because it means that you have been honest with him all along about your wants, your identity, and your contribution to your relationship.

CONFUSING HIM WITH YOUR CHANGE OF ATTITUDE

Fact: It will be easier for him to love you more if he knows that you are showing him your true colors from the start. No one wants to be deceived by a fake personality.

During the post-honeymoon discovery process, his perceptions of your personality "changes" could lead him to ask, "Who are you, and what did you do to my girlfriend?" He was attracted to you because of you, with your own set of quirks, temper, and passions. So where did those go?

It's a question of how real you were when you first met, what circumstances led you to meet him, and whether were you pretending to be someone else at the time. He could be suffering from the same malady; the propensity to take things at face value and not look beneath the surface. Your "other side" could confuse him and lead him to think that you tricked him into believing that you are someone else entirely.

If his perception of your "changes" is too extreme, do an objective self-analysis of what he saw or what side of your personality you showed him. In a long-term relationship, he will notice changes in your personality, but these aren't changes at all. That was you before you decided to adapt to some idea of who his ideal mate is

Sooner or later, your real personality will
this will confuse him. He might like th
he doesn't, try to look at how he will
want you to act a certain way to fit his i
girlfriend, or does he accept your personality a.
accordingly?

WHEN HE ASKS YOU TO CHANGE

Now, you're ready to take the plunge and start the real "getting-to-know-you" phase. Let's say that you allowed yourself a lot of space to modify some aspects of your personality initially to impress him. The problem now is introducing him to that side of you that he has never seen before. They say that love brings out the best in all of us, but what we have to know is that it could also bring out the worst. Rife with emotions, the relationship issues we deal with may reveal a side of our personality that could startle our partners, particularly when they don't see it coming.

If he asks you to change, you might find yourself at a point where you feel like running and staying at the same time. Reality can be harsh after you've been spoiled with honey-moon-period attention.

What do you do when he gets a glimpse of those sides of you that have been kept hidden during your initial stages as a couple, and decides that he doesn't want that kind of girl? What he'll do is first ask you to stick with what he's used to. He'll tell you that he doesn't like your style or your way of doing things now, and wonders why you're "changing."

Giving in to this kind of pressure and suppressing your true nature to please him is the easy way out. You could lose elf completely and won't have a clear picture of who are and what you want. You will lose your goals and ven your will to pursue things that may be part of your life's calling. You will be fooling him by changing a huge part of your personality, but not as much as you are fooling yourself.

What Exactly Does He Want to Change?

Not all changes are bad. There are instances when his intention is not to make you fit his notion of the perfect partner for him, but to encourage you to be the best that you can be. Partners like this are a find because they really care about your self-actualization and happiness in life. Take each criticism in stride and decide objectively whether you can do it or not, and whether you should.

Sometimes accepting a request to change can help you overcome a weakness. For example, after you have been dating for a while, he might ask you to be more domestically inclined. For years, you have been eating at the diner at the first floor. You have no idea how to start cooking or mixing things together to make a meal. It is not surprising that you did not reveal this fact to him while you were in your initial dating phases. If you live together or he comes to your place often, he will notice your hesitation to cook for him and this contributes to your insecurities. If you think that this change in your life will benefit you, why not go for it? Go to a cooking school and learn something. Better yet, experiment on your own and cook at home. His role, of course, is to eat anything you come up with.

You might also learn about maintaining a house. No, you won't turn into Martha Stewart overnight, but you can try to at least develop a good sense of which curtain colors hurt the eyes, and realize how wonderful it is to climb into a made bed at night. You'll know when it's time to change your cleaning habits when you feel uncomfortable about it.

If you feel comfortable with your sense of taste, however, tell him. You don't have to agree about every single item of clothing you own and he will soon get used to your umbrella hats, but the main point here is to take the suggestion constructively without losing your personal style. If you can rationalize why the rolls of tissue should be on the floor all the time, then you probably have very good reasons for keeping them there. Otherwise, take his suggestions (or complaints) as something that may make your quality of life better.

Small, constructive changes, like taking care of yourself more, learning how to maintain a house, learning how to cook, and developing budgeting skills are all good things. If he asks you to stop being a slob, why not do it? The object is to consider the implications of what he's asking from you. If it won't intrude into your sense of self and it won't permanently damage you psychologically, then do it.

Many self-improvement changes requested are for your own good, but remember that they resulted from taking good advice and nothing more. If you see the improvements as something that you did "for him," you could set yourself up for resentment.

Don't forget about the issue of reciprocity. If you accept his suggestions about cooking and cleaning the house more, you should also ask him to do away with his practice of leaving his trash everywhere. It's a fair give and take, which operates around the same idea of improving your lifestyle.

WHEN DOES ASKING FOR CHANGE EVOLVE INTO FORCING YOU TO CHANGE?

The small suggestions stated above are normal in relationships. These are small adjustments that you do to be able to live in harmony. There are, however, things in our lives that we cannot let go of as easily. These are principles that we grew up believing in, manifested in our daily lives, and shared with a lot of people we are close to.

These principles may have been taught to us through our religion, our culture, or through the environment that we grew up in. We may have complex belief systems that compose a big part of who we are. It represents the beliefs and principles of those who have come before us. We never outgrow these things and will even propagate these beliefs by teaching our children these same things in the future. They're principles that we take for granted that live inside the core of our being.

When a new beau asks you to give these principles up, it can mean war. For some of us, it's easy: Never date someone who does not share the same core beliefs. But what if the enigma called love targets two people who have different sets of beliefs? If the disparity is so great, tension is immediately felt when these issues are raised.

I am not saying that you should avoid a guy who does not believe in the same things you do, especially in terms of religious and cultural practices or cultural beliefs, but you should think long and hard before getting into a long-term relationship with a guy who shows signs of asking you to leave your church or family traditions in the future. If you think that your relationship is worth that kind of sacrifice, there are some things you will need to discuss with him. However, if you feel that turning your back on your culture and traditions will cause too much grief for you and your family, then changing your religion for him might just be a relationship deal-breaker.

Here are a few things to remember to maintain your sense of self in a relationship:

- **Reciprocity keeps things fair.** What if you give an inch and he rushes in to conquer a mile? Create walls to prevent the intrusion.

- **Change takes time.** Most changes do not come instantly, so he shouldn't expect you to do an instant overhaul and neither should you of him.

- **Change is tough.** He should recognize and appreciate that you are struggling with his expectations.

- **Sometimes change is not worth it.** Is he worth changing for? Consider your options and your priorities. If the adjustment takes away too much of who you are, maybe the relationship is not worth it.

COMPROMISE

If compromise were easy, the world would have fewer wars, be ten times cleaner and the economy would be in a lot better shape. Sadly, the whole process of compromise can go on for years and years, with global leaders and businesses adjusting only when crucial issues arise, rather than compromise a large part of their wealth, beliefs, and principles to make continual change for the better. A relationship is not much different. When a man and a woman opt to work things out rather than divorce or break up because of irreconcilable differences, they will soon realize just how compromises are made.

Above all, you can't force issues and you cannot rush compromise. The best you can do is hope that the other person does what he promised to do to make things better. Promising to change something is a two-way street, and it's usually done in baby steps. Most women expect a lot from their men, and vice versa, when it comes to change. It's not instant, so why rush it? There should be a time for a couple to give each other a progress report on their compromise. Find the best environment to discuss issues, and be in the best mood possible. Tell each other what you're having trouble dealing with so you can deal with it together.

ARE YOU HIS DOORMAT?

Some women find it extremely difficult to let go of a relationship that is obviously stuck in a rut and forces her to do away with a lot of what makes her the way she is. A woman develops trust for the man, regardless if it's misplaced or not.

So who knows best about what you need to do in this situation? Each woman involved in this type of unhealthy relationship knows the answer to this question, but just doesn't know how to give up the relationship. Either she thinks she won't meet another man who will be a better fit or she lacks the courage to stand firm in her beliefs.

The right man will respect you more if you remain firm with your convictions. They will serves as guides for him in dealing with you and making your relationship work. If he sees you as an equal and has a high regard for your capacity to think for yourself, he will be more supportive of your beliefs and more willing to compromise on issues in which you don't see eye to eye.

However, there are guys who truly think that they are right all of the time and take your refusal to follow their mandates as a sign of insubordination. When a woman gets bullied into acquiescing to everything her man wants, she willingly opens up herself to all kinds of abuse. Being able to defend your principles at least conveys the message of confidence. It will tell him in no uncertain terms that you will not just give in to anything he wants, that you can independently think of what's good for you, and that you are confident enough to stand up against him if he tries to dominate you.

So resist any urges to go for the easy way out. Puff up that chest and hold your head up high when you feel that you are in the right. Compromising a part of your principles should always give you a comfortable feeling in the end; you have studied everything and determined it to be good for you, prepared yourself for the compromise, and took the plunge. If you feel that you're only doing it to save your relationship and that you are grieving over your decision, do not compromise.

SETTING BOUNDARIES AND SPEAKING UP

Knowing how to compromise and deciding on which issues require compromise are cornerstones of a healthy relationship. If your man doesn't get it, explain it to him. You must always believe that you are pitching the best solution for the both of you to maintain happiness. He, in turn, should be able to logically react to your argument without shouting or verbal abuse.

Some people might feel that compromise is a weakness, but those who are unable to do so may are wallowing in emotional immaturity and cannot handle the best solutions that will foster mutual satisfaction. Breaking up becomes an option only if you have tried your very best to solve all issues with clear minds. Mutual respect, best intentions for each other, and untarnished honesty will go a long way in making your relationship work.

HOW TO BE IN CONTROL OF ISSUES THAT REQUIRE COMPROMISE

Confidence and compromise DO mix. In fact, the women who can compromise something are those who won't give everything they have just because someone asked. It speaks of high self-worth and of conquered insecurities. Deciding selectively what and what not to compromise on is a sign of high self-esteem, courage, and confidence. A confident person can sustain her self-worth even under fire or constant pressure from her partner. Confident women love themselves in a greater or similar way as they love their partners, and this strength puts them in the best position to make compromises.

A sure red flag displayed when your self-worth is low is the practice of thinking only about your past mistakes and missing the lessons in them. What usually follows an uncomfortable request to compromise is an inner tirade of "maybe he's right; I suck at this relationship thing and should just go along with what he wants me to do with myself."

How gracefully you handle pressure shows how much you value yourself and your capabilities to judge correctly. Focus on past problems that you solved successfully and the positive feelings that resulted. Love yourself unconditionally and let your love spill over to your partner and family, and you'll be able to get through any rough patches of compromise in a relationship successfully.

Chapter 7: Stop Over-Analyzing and Second-Guessing

girl meets boy and they like each other. Sometimes love is involved, but not always. It's hard to tell for a little while. Maybe you'll have a few more dates, and maybe your last date was your last. How can you really tell how things are going?

Second-guessing a guy's intentions can lead you to setting yourself up for disillusionment. On the other hand, ignoring red flags could lead to disappointment. There's a big difference between staying cool in a relationship and being clueless.

Let's say you went on a date after several weeks of wonderful online chat, and you can't wait to see how the two of you fare offline. The first date was fun and there seems to be a lot of chemistry. You were both so swept away by the moment that you both decided to go for it. The motel downtown seemed a haven of romance and love that night, and none of you had any regrets. The future looks promising … right? That's when the mind games start.

There's a lot of guess work involved in new relationships. How relationship milestones are handled during this phase will contribute to the tenacity of the relationship. While sex too early can kill a budding relationship, it seemed like the right thing to do because both partners felt that it was the right thing to do at the time. The problem with sex between two partners who barely know each other, however, is that it brings up a lot of questions. Was it just sex? Will we always have sex when we meet up because we started our relationship with sex?

The magic that occurred that night happened because you let it. It is just that, magic. It's fun, enjoyable, and extremely gratifying, but it doesn't mean that you have to let that feeling extend to reality. The first date is always a spring-board to better things, Yes, the sex could have proven what you suspected all along, that your chemistry is amazing. However, this is hardly a basis for everlasting love; or even love that will extend beyond that first time together.

There's a good chance that sex will always be the topic of your next conversations after that fateful night, because that's mostly what you know you have in common at this point. The trouble starts when colorful sexual conversations are all that you have.

IF IT SEEMS LIKE IT'S GOING TOO FAST, IT PROBABLY IS

Delusions of him liking or loving you already could mean trouble, especially when the reality is that he's still just checking you out. Remember that love at first sight is a wonderful theory, usually professed at the altar when a man and woman finally say their I-dos. It's romantic to say that you fell in love at first sight to friends and family when you have already secured the future together, but it's not so real-istic when conquering your "morning-after" feelings.

Of course it's not always the girl's fault that she falls for the guy easily. Some men have the gift of gab. They will flirt with you, wrap you around clouds of fairy dust, and sweep you away with sweet nothings and touchy-feely behavior. Like you, he could be into savoring those romantic moments before the magic ends.

Sadly, the magic does not end for some girls. They assume that the guy has the best intentions, thinking up baseless assumptions that could lead to delusions, and saying yes in their minds before he even asks.

WAKE-UP CALL

Before you proceed with falling in love with him prematurely and hitting rock bottom in the empty well of early unrequited relationship romance, listen up. Some gestures are simply done out of flirting or habit and don't necessarily mean he's head-over-heels in love with you like you are with him. Find time to breathe after the first date, taking things as they come, and concentrating on friendship before assuming love.

Aim for friendship. Say hello cordially and warmly but do not go overboard. If he wants to discuss the sex, you can allow yourselves a recap, but try to vary the topic to something else so that you can discover some other things you might have in common. Find another common ground besides great sex. Having great sex during the first date means you can now go on without the sexual tension, so use that excuse to get to know each other on a non-sexual level. Who knows, there could be something there in the far future, when you've both become accustomed to each other's company.

Second-guessing his actions when you know so little of him or his personality could lead to disappointments. Bear in mind that if you blow up at him during the first week after that first date, you are headed for heartbreak hill.

Above all, do not call, e-mail, or IM him to ask (again) if it was just sex, or if there is "something else." The fastest way to scare a guy off is to force a relationship out of him when you barely know each other. You don't even know if this intrusion (yes he will see it as an intrusion) is welcome. If he's a nice guy, he might tell you not to expect too much from him directly, particularly if he regarded your experience as a very hot date and nothing more. A man may also not want to hurt your feelings and will try to let you down gently, slowly and over time.

If he is like most men, however, he will enjoy the attention, with or without the intention of stringing you along. It is flattering to have someone adore you so much, and for a while he could feel the same. The problem is you have just met each other and have just made love, so rational thinking is not exactly at the forefront.

When talking over the phone, keep your cool and use your senses to listen to pauses. Professing your love over and over and expecting him to answer "I love you too" will put the strain on your new relationship. Love is something that develops over time, not overnight.

DOES HE FEEL LIKE YOU'RE JUMPING HIM EMOTIONALLY?

It's more than a bit presumptive to think that one night of hot sex sealed the deal. When you listen to locker room conversation, you will realize how many guys run from clingy girls. Most guys want to call the shots and do the courting, and they like coming up against a challenge that doesn't come with unnecessary emotional grief. If you were too forward with a guy and he ran, you crossed over into the clingy category. He probably won't even tell you why he's no longer interested, and now you're second guessing your way to finding an answer. Or, you start dialing…

THE CALL

Do any of these statements look familiar to you?

"He didn't call!"

"He stopped calling!"

"When is he going to call me?"

Modern technology is amazing. We can contact people several ways in an instant, and yet waiting for that call, e-mail, or SMS, or IM ping can feel like forever, and when it does come in, it can get hopes up for relationships that never happen. Half of the time after a date, a girl is dreamily looking forward to the call, and the other half is spent thinking that he will never call. When he does call, it's like the magic is happening all over again.

Relationships have ended and started with just a single phone call. Everything starts with that fated question—"When is he going to call me?—and waiting becomes the call-me curse that can only be escaped with another call.

It's more than hope that keeps women waiting for the call, it's the inability to accept that he isn't feeling the way she is. Didn't he tell her that she was wonderful? Now it seems that her sanity and her emotional stability depend on one phone call from a guy who, a few days before their date, never existed in her life. After a few days, she might get impatient. Her sleep-deprived, mind-muddled brain starts the delusion.

Let's say that the guy did say "I'll call you, OK?" as he rode away in his car. This vague promise would have been stronger if he had mentioned a date and the exact time that he will call. It takes a really cloudy mind not to notice, but at that moment, she wasn't feeling at all rational.

The real issue isn't his promise of call; it's the woman's assumption that he cares enough to keep that promise because he feels the same way she does. We can't even blame it on the romantic movies and other media that told her about sincere love after a hook-up, because after a few days of silence, she'll still be hanging on to the dream even though it's clear that it's pure fantasy.

At this truly deluded start rationalizing theoretical excuses for why he hasn't called:

> *"He must have lost my number; maybe I should I call him."*

> *"I knew I should not have talked to Bessie all night—what if he's been calling and the phone was busy?"*

> *"He could be on vacation or maybe his work schedule might be really tight."*

While the lack of communication is probably good wake-up call of its own to not make excuses for the silence anymore, it all starts over when he calls again.

There are nice guys who keep their promises to call back, though, but its still doesn't mean they're into you the same way you're into them yet. So these calls aren't the times to fawn over him, either. Keep your cool. Assuming that he feels the same longing is a mistake. In fact, he could be dating several people. But let's give the guy the benefit of the doubt and look at his reasons for calling you again.

He could be reminiscing about the hot time you got it on and might want a repeat performance. Or maybe he remembers that you flirted with him, gave him the come-on, and it was hot. Or he could be showing his appreciation by not dropping you like a hot potato right after a hot night together. Even when he was acting very cordial and appreciative of your attention, he could be looking for the nicest way to tell you that he's not ready. In either of these cases you might think he's into you on a potential long-term relationship level, but in reality he doesn't expect anything from you besides pleasure.

This extra-nice-to-you response could be involuntary, and doesn't mean anything for now. One example of this is when he sees a girl hailing a cab under a torrent of rain and he has his car with him. His instinct would be to help the girl out and offer a ride. This doesn't mean that he likes the girl already, it just means he is doing a good deed because his conscience won't let him just drive by—and she might be attractive.

Yes, curiosity comes into play. He's interested because he is attracted to you, and asked you out to get to know you better. Every gesture and action during the date could be very nice and all that, but he will still have to decide in the end if he still wants to date you in the future. Getting your hopes up after the initial "very intense" date is normal, but assuming a lasting relationship with him based on the fun you had during that time is unrealistic.

Preemptive assumptions destroy everything, even friendship. He will get turned off that you're reading too much into his friendly actions and stop doing them completely.

Unless he makes it perfectly clear that he wants to pursue a relationship with you, a reality check is needed after every date, conversation, and every time he calls you "baby."

Let's face it, he could really be a very friendly guy, and the special way he treats you might be the same way that he treats all his friends. Observe how he is with his other friends. Does he do the same things for them? If he is a naturally sweet gentleman, he treats all women this way. What you think is "special treatment" could be his way of showing that you are his friend, too.

See how it goes, take everything in stride. He might be biding his time before he really pops the relationship question. Patience will get you where you want to be, if it's meant to be. For now, preserve your dignity by not reading too much between the lines. .

IF HE DIDN'T INTEND FOR ME TO FALL FOR HIM WHY DOESN'T HE JUST SAY SO?

Some men are bad seeds that like attention but don't give back what the woman deserves. However, believe it or not, there are guys who go out of their way to be nice to women who are obviously smitten with them. Consider yourself lucky if you guy belongs to the latter type. That he hasn't said "bug off" yet or simply blown you off is his way of observing if you will actually snap out of it soon. He liked you and it's obvious because he is still talking to you, but make no mistake; right now he really wants to be friends.

He can't give up on an interesting girl, even if she seems to be under the illusion that he wants more from her.

So, how does a girl start over when she's professed love at first sight already? She has to figure out how to look at this guy in a new light, and this time without acting through the hazy cloud of potential love inside her head.

1. **Get a new hobby, or anything else that will get your mind off him.** The less you communicate, the more he can breathe easy that you are not the cloyingly sweet and possibly delusional girl that he saw the morning after your first date.

2. **Really get to know him.** Give yourself your own "What the hell was I thinking?" moment and just reflect on how you fell for the guy. Dig deeper into his personality and talk to him about the topics you care about. You could be surprised that you really do not have anything in common with him.

3. **Save the Drama.** Post a note on your dresser that says "Men don't want heart-wrenching drama." Give him time to miss you, court you even. Do not over-react, overanalyze, and overrate him. When your head is clear of the fantasy you have created you will see him as he really is and this could be just what he's been waiting for. Face it; you don't like drama in the workplace because you cannot function properly. You'd sooner send in a resignation letter than be forced to endure three-hour breaks daily for a year with your boss who's been crying over an office affair she had. Drama isn't productive, and it stalls you from your objectives. Your guy feels the same way.

ASK YOUR FRIENDS FOR A REALITY CHECK

Your friends know you and how you are when you're into a guy. Ask them honestly if they think you're over-analyzing things with your new "somewhat boyfriend." Better yet, pick the most in-your-face person within your group and describe your relationship so far with the guy. Shelve your subjective, romance novel-like account of what happened and lay down the facts. Don't say, "His eyes looked into mine and I knew he was also in love with me" or "When his hands touched mine, I felt him shudder."

Their opinions may be hard to hear because they slap you back to reality and make you uncomfortable about the feelings or notions that brought all the second guessing on in the first place. But, remember that when a guy says one thing and does another, he was pulling your leg. Sometimes, it takes a lot of shaking from friends to really think about your mistakes in assessing relationships with men.

DON'T SAY YOU'RE READY FOR A CASUAL RELATIONSHIP IF YOU REALLY CAN'T HANDLE IT

One of the most exasperating contradictions men deal with when is being involved with a woman who claims she wants their relationship to stay casual but comes across as the clingy, relationship-hungry girl that she is. If the relationship was truly casual, she wouldn't fling things across the room whenever he talked about anything that could be loosely translated to "another girl." After all, if she agreed to a casual relationship in the first place, a girl has no right to complain.

Women agree to an open relationship or the friends-with-benefits relationship, but deep inside, they are absolutely sure he will see the light over time. As long as she keeps making him feel important to her, making sure he's OK every few minutes and keeps on reminding him that he exists, soon he will realize how much she means to him, right?

Wrong! He will only feel confused and guilty when you get hurt and cry that he's being "unfair" despite his playing by the casual, open-relationship rules that you agreed to. The rule that you're breaking is to say what you mean and mean what you say. No mind games need be played because you are supposed to be honest to each other as friends who sleep together. If you are feeling that you love him, he could tell, and you're better off telling him anyway so that he knows how to react accordingly. Waiting for a friends-with-benefits relationship to change into something more may be a fruitless effort regardless.

Some guys feel pressured by the "boyfriend" label. It is the modern-day equivalent of fiancé for guys, and they avoid it like the plague. Ask yourself if you really want the kind of guy who rushes after an adventure then sprints back to his solitude when things get sticky? Opening your eyes to what he really is all about will reveal all the stuff that you didn't see when you were wrapped up in him.

THE BASICS OF KEEPING IT REAL

- **Practice sound mind over raging heart.** If this guy was with another friend, would you consider him a good catch for her?

- **Keep it in perspective.** Know that he is only one guy and putting him at the center of your world and assuming that he's doing the same to you could be a waste of time. Use this time to increase your self-confidence and meet other men.

- **Using selective blinders is blinding.** Try to see more than only what you want to see. Open up those five senses and remove the blindfold. What did you see in him anyway?

- **Learn how to identify red flags.** With your five sense open and objective, are there any glaring warning signs that you may have missed before?

Red Flags

It's easy to miss warning signals through the love-dovey haze, especially if his words belie his actions. But there are healthier ways to second-guess this new guy in your life, like analyzing how he is with his past girlfriends. Notice the way he talks about them frequently—or infrequently. This is one of many key points that could serve as warning signs that should alert a girl to focus more on what he's saying than what she thinks he's saying. These signs could indicate a troubled relationship in the future.

Even if there are red flags, though, he could still be the man for you in the long run. Still, it's good to keep an eye on what a man reveals about himself during the early stages when you're still in that "one of the girls he went out with for a while" category. Here are some key red-flag issues to watch for:

- **Relationship durations and reasons.** You might notice how he glosses over how and why past breakups occurred. Resist overt prying and let him to blab for a while. You might be surprised what he tells you.

- **Divorce.** If he claims to be over his divorce, yet mentions this fact several times in the conversation that ensues, or accidentally calls you by her name—it happens!—he could still be in denial.

- **One-way communication opportunities.** He won't give you his landline, but asks for all your contact info. This is the ultimate red flag and could mean trouble with privacy or other relationships he may be hiding from you.

- **Leads you on.** Fans your love-at-first sight theory yet stays out of sight for days or weeks at a time. If he's stringing you along for the monthly cheat session, wise up and realize what it is.

- **Chronically "between jobs."** For how long? (So, who's paying for this hotel stay then?!?)

- **The Saturday-night caller.** He professes his love for you over the phone after a week of non-communication, and it's Saturday. Is he drinking and dialing? Think of why he's really calling. Could it be because he couldn't find another Saturday girl for that week?

Chapter 8: Mr. Perfect or Mr. Right?

encouraged by the media's hype on the quest for Mr. Perfect, some ladies have made that guy their benchmark for choosing a potential boyfriend. Honestly, a genuine guy with a few flaws makes a better boyfriend choice than spending your time looking for a Mr. Perfect that does not exist. Mr. Right Now could turn out to be Mr. Right-For-You—and happens to live next door or work in the next cubicle, not in some chateau in the south of France.

THE PROCESS OF FALLING IN LOVE

Analyzing the way you respond to men will make you realize your patterns in being attracted to individuals who posses a significant portion of the "Mr. Perfect" traits you have always associated with the perfect guy for you. These traits come from preconceived notions of who we want to be with for the rest of our lives. This theoretical guy has everything we need and none of the flaws that we hate. He will be handsome, rich, with a stable job, sensitive to our needs, and very emotionally available. He will be there whenever we want romance, and will shower us with the love that we have always craved.

By that all-encompassing definition, of course he won't be like the guys we see on a daily basis. Those men, like us, are flawed. They can be slobs who take the easy way out of everything and may forget very important dates like birthdays and anniversaries. They will often be unavailable for dates, and might only be able to afford going out on paydays. These imperfect guys are everywhere, but in their midst is the perfect guy.

It's pretty difficult for a normal guy to compete with the theoretical guy you are already in love with who represents everything that you want in a partner. How can the Average Joe possibly fulfill your numerous requirements, when you have already decided that he isn't good enough for you?

A woman who is already in love with Mr. Perfect or Mr. Right goes through a process of falling in love with someone who might fit the bill. The amazing thing is that a woman often deems a guy "perfect" during their initial meeting and the short encounters that follow only because she turns a blind eye to his faults.

You may be attracted to some men who show one trait that you have on your list. Then you stay long enough to find out if that same guy shows all the other things you are looking for. You prepare a mental checklist as you look him over, smiling wider each time he says something that reinforces your belief that he is "The One."

Here are the three main categories of what attracts us to another:

- **Physical Appearance.** How he dresses and grooms himself is the first thing that others notice. A person who is pleasant to look at will be hard to resist and will demand attention from someone who is looking for that particular trait.

- **Attraction to Personality.** We are amazed by the easy way a guy can draw us into a conversation; and the way he exudes an aura of confidence.

- **Attraction to Intellect.** Women are fascinated with the way a guy formulates ideas in his brain and how deeply he regards things.

The fact is some women won't give the average guy a second look because they are reserving all their emotions for their imagined prince, the guy they are sure they are meant to be with. And yet, an Average Joe who has everything they could ever want in a partner could be right in front of them.

REDEFINING MR. PERFECT AND MR. RIGHT

Here's a wake-up call: Mr. Perfect does NOT exist!

If you base your relationship search on something as delusional as the "perfect man," you will end up with nothing and no one in the end. You aren't perfect yourself, so why would you put pressure on your guy to be perfect? The sooner a woman realizes that the image of someone "who has everything and good manners, too" is just a figment of her imagination, the sooner she can move on and meet the great men who may just show the real qualities she is looking for, without the unrealistic fluff.

Joanna made the choice to get over Mr. Perfect and start dating again:

When I finally accepted that I will never meet the perfect guy, I felt amazingly free—free to explore possibilities and free to take risks by going on dates that my friends set up for me. Now, I know that some men are attractive in the not-so-perfect way and each has something else to be proud of. I have always been too afraid to take risks that could scar me forever. I wanted to be untarnished so that when the perfect guy finally comes along, I could pour out all the longing that I kept inside.

I'm now free to meet men with imperfections, who may or may not have the exact things I really look for in a man, but who cares? I'm having fun talking about anything, hearing them talk about their jobs they love but won't make them a fortune, joking around with them about really silly topics that would generally would not have appealed to the man of my dreams (because they're so silly).

While some of the same issues and "what-ifs" that have kept me from dating for the past few years still exist, I have now learned to believe that somehow it will all work out in the end, even if the man I share my future with is not the millionaire, debonair macho guy, or the ultra-romantic guy that I initially thought I needed to be happy.

I finally found out that not having an image in my mind of how I want my partner to look and act made me open up as a person. Maybe it's time to examine what it is I really want for myself in the long run. Finally, life is opening up for me and who knows— I might even fall in love.

MANY MEN ARE EMOTIONALLY AVAILABLE BUT DON'T GET NOTICED

The Mr. Perfect trend has ruined the chances of some average men. How can they show a girl what they can offer in a committed relationship when girls don't even glance in their direction? Digging deeper and going beyond the physical could reveal a gem of a personality and the kind of person who could make you happy for a lifetime. Beneath the material things the wealth of sensitive love that he is willing to share with you makes him a great catch. Behind the seemingly "ordinary façade" lies a gentleman who will make you feel like the princess that you are. He comes not with jewels and grand promises but great companionship and an extraordinary wit. The most important thing to consider in a man is that he goes out of his way to make you feel special.

WILL YOU SETTLE FOR A MR. RIGHT-FOR-YOU?

When you're in a relationship with an extraordinary Mr. Right Now, how can you tell that he's, in fact, Mr. Right?

You might have thought previously that all men you've encountered were wrong for you, and wondered whether the "Mr. Rights" that your friends and colleagues have landed were actually manufactured somewhere in a special factory in a secret location. They seem to be happy, so what's wrong with all of the guys you've met?

Take a minute and suppose that it hasn't been the guy that's been "wrong," but maybe that anybody would become Mr. Wrong when judged against your impossible standards. Many women fall for men for the wrong reasons. When it comes to finding a great relationship, many women willingly walk in blinded by the "perfection" that they initially see, only to find that the men they choose don't turn out to be the princes they thought them to be.

So, what's the best way of finding Mr. Right? When differentiating a Mr. Right Now and a Mr. Right, make a list of the things you want in a partner. Be realistic and for once, do not put in anything that relates to the material or physical. Instead, focus on positive, inner qualities that he has. No one's saying that appearance isn't important to a degree, but as age comes and the body withers, you'll want to be with someone who still excites you and makes you feel good with the kind of traits that come from the heart.

ESSENTIAL QUALITIES TO LOOK FOR IN A MAN

When searching for a man who is good for you, you must look for some non-negotiable conditions that need to be there in someone before you start a relationship with them. These include a stable job, psychological stability (e.g., not a drug addict), and at communication skills that are at least open enough to get his message of affection across. He must inspire you to keep doing well in your job, and he must be at least open to the idea of having a family someday, if that's what you are seeking.

The physical traits are the icing on the cake in your quest for the best guy for you. He must be presentable enough to make you feel comfortable being around him. Maybe he isn't built like a football player, but he's cuddly enough and the feel of his arms around you makes you swoon. Remember that beauty is in the eyes of the beholder and your standards for good looks need not match those of the airbrushed male models and actors you see on the silver screen.

Once you've established your non-negotiable list, you can trim it down some more to what you really need in your life. Make sure you examine all your existing assumptions to really assess which conditions are really important right now those that wouldn't really matter in the long run.

When I was younger, I wanted a prince who was handsome, rich, and lived in a castle. I grew up believing that he really existed. During early adulthood I realized that I could do away with the castle and would settle for a red Ferrari instead. Now that I have lost the magical idealism of youth, what I look for in a guy is much simpler and can be summarized in a few words: I want a guy who will love me unconditionally.

DECIDING WHICH CHARACTERISTICS YOU WANT IN A MAN

Next, create a list of characteristics that you would like in a partner. Here you may use the lessons you have learned from your other relationships and friendships. It may help to think of your best guy friends as models for some of the things that could work for you. Our guy friends are wonderful advisors when it comes to relationship issues. Because they're our friends, the chemistry isn't there so you can connect with them in a different level, almost like a brother.

Looks fade with time, and the heart of a person is where all the goodness comes. When you find yourself choosing a guy for his heart and kindness towards you and those you love, you will be happier and more content than when you choose someone who may have more issues than you in terms of vanity and ego. Think of the quality of life you want in the future, even if "forever" seems far off.

Here's a sample list:

- Willing to work and capable of working for a living

- Dependable

- Able to relax when it's time to relax

- Respects your beliefs even when you're from different backgrounds

- Has a good heart and will help out those in need

- Is affectionate in many different ways.

- Respects your freedom and your privacy

- Comfortable around children

Is there someone in your past that fits the bill, but you didn't give him a second glance because he lacks material and physical qualities that you were looking for in a guy then? Do old boyfriends and past lovers have more than a few of these characteristics? What attracted you to them in the first place? How many of their traits match your list of needs?

If there is little correlation between what you need and the types of men you meet, maybe you are looking in the wrong places. Simply wishing that the right guys will find you somehow is not enough, so position yourself to give the guys that display your list of desired qualities an opportunity to meet you. It also helps to show the same characteristics you value yourself to them.

There is that theory that a woman can attract the man she wants by showing the same qualities she desires in him herself. Like attracts like, and if you truly want to meet someone who lives up to a set of standards you may have, you need to attain those on your own to truly attract what you desire. One way to find a similar-minded man is to share the same activities.

FINDING SOMEONE NEW

Knowledge of what you want in a man before you start actively looking for love aids in separating the good from the not-so-good, and the best from the worst. However, you should give each person you meet the benefit of the doubt. He may not look like the guy in your mind, but he may show a sterling heart. Your goal is to achieve compatibility in your relationship, and to explore the possibility of lasting love.

ONE SINGLE WOMAN'S SEARCH FOR THE RIGHT GUY

A woman who advertises her availability in the proper way will find that there are a lot more men who are like her looking for someone who can fill their relationship void. A lot of decent single men are in this for the long haul, but they are just waiting for the right woman.

One single girl joined a singles party in the hopes of finding new friends:

> *It's difficult to be alone in a room full of strangers. Being thrust in a place away from your usual support group makes it necessary for you to find ways to cope with the stress of putting yourself out there to meet new people. Is this really necessary? Is this the right place to find a man that shows all the qualities I want?*

Some people get their love fix from single dates that don't go anywhere, but what this girl wants is the kind of companionship that forms with a friend and a lover in one. A relationship that goes beyond a one-night stand is something not talked about on the first date—and you should run if it is—but it is implied or hoped for. The best way to start a lasting relationship is to "hook up" with men who see more than the physical. This will undoubtedly take longer than a one-night stand that rushes relationships too quickly, but the payoff in the long run is so much more worth it if you're looking for the kind of love to last a lifetime.

> *Since I've been here, I've done a little bit of looking and talking. But when things go really, really wrong and my mood can't get any lower, what else can I do but grab a coffee and hope that he'll find me?*

WHEN WOMEN DECIDE TO STICK WITH MR. WRONG

Sometime girls stick to their rut relationships because they hang on too tight to the belief that they have found their Mr. Perfect: someone who looks exactly like the man of their dreams superficially. But these women didn't bank on the fact that these men have issues beneath that sparkling surface that need a lot of work. At first, the woman, of course, is willing to try to make it work for the sake of her relationship with the perfect guy she was lucky enough to snag.

Here are typical scenarios that women encounter when they're clearly with Mr. Wrong:

- **Looks belie reality.** You thought he had everything, but after a little while you find yourself doubting the qualities you thought were in him to begin with. Still, you ignore his uncouth behavior and the beginnings of what could be verbal abuse that comes from this guy, believing that he must be "The One" because you look "perfect" together.

- **Other guys look better.** You see and know other men who you know would be much better for you in terms of satisfying your need for peace of mind, affection, and a good everyday laugh, but you ignore them because you have already invested a lot of your time and attention in your guy. You concentrate instead on wishing that he'd be more emotionally available and would appreciate you more. Besides, you know for a fact that all the other girls are eating their hearts out in envy.

- **Everything is for him.** You spend a lot of your time and resources to keep your perfect guy interested, but why does it feel like he thinks he deserves all the attention? When will he shower attention on you like you do for him?

- **Friends give him the thumbs down.** Your most trusted friends reveal that they have misgivings about your continued infatuation with this guy and all tell you that he's not the right one for you. You ignore their advice because you intend to make your relationship work, no matter what.

- **He's incorrigible.** When he gets into a tiff with someone, you know deep inside that his behavior is unacceptable but you don't say anything because it might offend him. You listen patiently to how he rationalizes his role as the victim, but secretly wish that you could say something that will shed a more realistic light on the situation. But afraid to show him your disappointment lest he turn on you, you keep your mouth shut.

Unfortunately, a lot of girls are unable to let go of fitting the wrong guy to play the starring role in the fairytale playing in their heads, even in the face of evidence. If they did, they'd find a guy who won't make them feel like tending to the relationship is the worst chore in the world. These types of women progress from rut relationships to rut marriages, and spend a lot on counseling sessions (IF they can convince the guy to go).

There are women who create their own fairytales, not with princes but with frogs with golden hearts—and they get to live them in their daily lives. The best relationships are built on understanding of each other's needs. Those who get this straight at the onset will enjoy the fruits of a compatible union.

How Do You Know If He's "The One"?

The right guy for you is supportive and encourages you from pursuing the things you love to do. When priorities conflict, he will say what's on his mind, but he will always allow you to do what you think is best.

Likewise, you can accept him and his goals for your relationship because you understand clearly what they are, and he will never try to overhaul your personality to fit his needs. He listens compassionately when you rant, and laughs with you at mistakes, rather than use you as his fall guy (or fall girl). He is stern when you deviate from the relationship path that you agreed on, but not too stern that he doesn't listen to your explanation as to why you made that turn. He trusts your judgment and accepts that you can make mistakes, too.

He loves you for you, and who you were before he met you. He doesn't judge your family and friends and he won't make you leave those that you love for him. He won't be selfish with your time, yet reminds you time and time again that he appreciates all the time you are giving to him. He goes out of his way to be nice to your family and wouldn't mind spending some time with them.

You both make time for each other, even when your schedules are tight. He plans for your quality time together and looks forward to it like an excited kid waiting for Christmas.

One crucial compatibility that must exist between you is sharing a similar belief system. You don't have to share the same religion, but you do have to accept each other's philosophies. Spirituality is something that is not taken lightly, and if he understands this, he will not laugh derisively at you when you do things that satisfy you on a spiritual level.

The "Perfect" front is an amazing lure, but you will have to go beyond that to really get the best quality of life you deserve.

Chapter 9: Stay True To Who You Are,
But Also Stay Open

If you have spent years focusing on yourself—working through your emotional issues, taking care of your body, and building your career success bit by bit, you are deserving of a partner who is right there on your level. The thing is, sometimes men are a bit overwhelmed by a strong woman. Also, there are times when strong women don't give certain men a chance because, on the surface they don't seem to be your equal. How can you deal with a man who is intimidated by you? How do you adjust your thinking and give the "average guy" a chance?

Today we live in a society in which women are empowered more than ever before. Many top positions across numerous fields are filled by women and it is now acceptable when they excel in different ways. From female presidents to female kick-boxing champions, it is not surprising that some women who feel that they have achieved the best in their field of expertise will tend to look for men who are on a similar level. A lot of these successful single women are completely happy being married to their work or careers, but there are those who still secretly yearn for a fruitful relationship when they are away from the prying eyes of workplace critics.

THE STRONG WOMAN

Billy Joel's classic song "She's Always a Woman" heaves a sigh to most single and strong female listeners, as those lyrics really hit home. They paint a portrait of the modern woman, the girl who can hold her own in the workplace and in any other environment she chooses. Her management style is quite different from her male counterparts. With a woman's intuition she can sense when something is not going as planned and isn't shy about letting others know how she feels about any deviations from a plan she labored long and hard to put into place.

Because female bosses have been regarded in the past as soft, many women must project a stiff character on the exterior who must surpass the perception of others' expectations. She has squelched all innuendo thrown at her through her actions that disprove that gender was ever a weakness. She may have a soft spot for something, but whatever it is, it isn't present all the time because she is all business, all results, and all goals—all the time. Everyone bows to her. She is firm in conviction and extremely aware of the machismo culture that is prevalent in most environments.

The battle of the sexes has waged long before women's liberation and even today under the blanket of fair play and competition on allegedly equal footing. So it is not surprising that women who have reached very high positions in their chosen fields are subjected to negative stereotypes. These stereotypes are so rampant that women of substance have struggled and fought these by either ignoring them completely, or by shooting down any suggestive innuendo that might pertain to these stereotypes.

While trying to project as much toughness as possible to gain respect all the time, how can a strong woman find a great date who will satisfy all her requirements without intimidating him? The truth is if a guy knows what's good for him, he will approach the strong woman and not wait for her to chase him. She is a catch, and has worked so hard to get where she is. Any guy should know that.

WHY SOME GUYS HESITATE TO PURSUE STRONG WOMEN

Believe it or not, some guys are actually scared of dating strong women. They have their own inferiorities and will see your potential disdain for them as worse than "normal" rejection from women who are not as strong. So they won't risk it, no matter how much they men want to date you.

Most men like girls they can "get" without shedding blood, though a lot of men respond to a woman's dominance well. It has something to do with how they were raised. They have dealt with a dominant woman all their lives—their mothers.

Sadly, the fear of approaching this type of women can be debilitating to some men. No one wants to be shot down, and no one wants to spend a lot of time going after a girl who may not even look at him twice because he is way below her perceived status.

Even those who may feel qualified to date you because they, too, worked their way to the top of the career ladder, may be hesitant to court you because they fear they'll lose their nerve or they instantly tag you as "high maintenance."

He'll end up ditching the notion of asking you out because he feels that you won't be receptive to someone who is not your superior in everything. And when every single guy you know has this attitude towards you, your chance at getting dates becomes slimmer.

ARE YOU *REALLY* OUT OF ANYONE'S LEAGUE?

When you give off the vibe that your standards are really high, everyone thinks that you are out of their league.

The "league" system in relationships seems fairly convoluted. In our minds, we tend to categorize people into leagues based on age, physical attractiveness, intellectual quotient, religion, and line of work. Dating someone who you deem higher or lower than you depends on which standards you base your assumption.

Making it clear to your potential dates that you have very high standards that he could not hope to meet is tantamount to never getting asked to go out again at all. A lot of guys are wimps when it comes to facing rejection; thoughts of not being good enough for you will cross their minds. Your whole attitude of close-mindedness when it comes to choosing dates will scare off even the bravest souls who might consider asking you out.

Some say that dating out of your league will only lead to heartbreak, and some even go as far to say that people should stick to their "own kind." But when we stop thinking of leagues or categories, we realize that every person is unique and special. What is it about that new guy that you just met that sets him apart from the rest of the guys you met in the past? What is he passionate about?

Being genuinely interested in a guy without letting your perception of leagues cloud your judgment will increase your market value and will make you more desirable.

HOW TO BE MORE APPROACHABLE TO MEN

You are a challenge, and a lot of your colleagues know it. Being single and at the top could be lonely, so most of your admirers will readily offer to accompany you there. Some of these men could be regular Joes who know of your standards but will still be willing to try to date you because of several things:

- **Curiosity.** *What is she like when she's out of the cutthroat work environment?*

- **Admiration**. *Man, I bet she's one helluva conversationalist!*

- **Confidence** that he can offer you something that you'd be interested in. *She's single, I'm single, so why not?*

Showing a soft side could get you closer to finding the kind of man who can offer you more than you ever hoped for. You know about your softer side, but not everyone does so be prepared to show your feminine side to men you find attractive and admire.

Invite your colleagues, bosses, and subordinates who could be harboring some doubts about your ability to socialize on a personal level to a relaxing team-building event that takes place on a beach or at a great coffee shop. This outing will be your chance to show how you are when completely relaxed and having fun. This also allows them to look at you in another way. Yes, they may still be intimidated by you because of your high standards, but now they know that you can be approached. It opens up the door.

DO NOT WEAR YOUR COAT
WHEN IT'S NOT NEEDED

If you remember the Tom Cruise flick, *Top Gun*, there's a scene there that showed how differently the young Maverick Mitchell reacted around his hot woman professor when he didn't know what she did for a living. In the movie, the woman acted professionally while in class but dropped the "boss" aura when she was just hanging out with her students in the bar.

Meeting someone new can be challenging and questions like "What do you do for a living?" come up quite often. You can choose to answer these questions objectively and briefly without putting on airs and going all out in mentioning your list of achievements, which progressively turns most quality men off. Even men with a room full of trophies of their own will not appreciate being subjected to the stories of a braggart. Yes, even though you're aiming to impress him and express your caliber to him to see if there's a good fit, he will see your incessant self-promotion as bragging. Even if he seems interested, he won't appreciate talking about what you do, how successful you are, and what you hope to achieve in the next five years for the majority of your time together.

Drop the pompousness and concentrate on the obvious fact. You're a single girl, and he's a single guy. You aren't trying to pitch a marketing strategy or a new research break-through, so talk about something else. Women who spent their whole lives going after a position in a company or perfecting their techniques in their chosen careers will not find it difficult to talk about other things if they focus on who they are talking to and not on themselves. Ask him questions about neutral things, and if you met this guy in a special environment, like a hobby center, talk about the hobby that you both share.

Your conversation could branch out to other things, and he will realize that your 'substance' comes from the fact that you can maintain a conversation with someone who doesn't care about the billions of dollars that your department has managed to bring in last year.

THE "AVERAGE GUY"

The notion of what's only "average" is very subjective. Someone you regard as average may be regarded differently in other circles. People have strengths that are more obvious in certain environments and not so obvious in others. For example, someone who is an outdoorsman may feel "out of place" in Wall Street, but in his natural niche, he is an authority. A guy who holds a regular job may be a wiz at time management and may be able to get through a day of multitasking effectively.

There are some women who completely feel entitled to have a man that, by social definition, is a good catch and refuse to give an "average" guy a chance.

Judging a person based on what he does for a living is not uncommon. We associate a person's strength with what they do in society, how they contribute, and how they earn their money. However, if we strip the titles and the ranks from everyone we know, we are able to see them as they are: people who work for a living, who may manage their priorities differently, and who may be able to complement other people's personalities by being the yang to their yin.

A woman should give a guy she deems as "average" a chance to get to know her better. In the process, she might even discover that her standards and notions of which type of guy fits her best could be skewed. The very basics of relationships revolve around how we can interact on different levels with people from different backgrounds. Openness to others' opinions is still the best way to find the person to share your life with.

WHAT IF THEY'RE TOO INTIMIDATED TO APPROACH?

If you feel that it's beneath you to ask a guy out, think again. It only seems "too forward" if the invitation isn't phrased correctly. The idea is to make it seem like he asked you. This translates to giving him an opening of some sort, an opportunity to ask you. Phrase your invitation as a question or open-ended comment to effectively pass the ball to him. Try something like, *"I wonder what it's like having dinner by the beach this time of the year"* or *"That movie looks like a lot of fun. What do you think?"*

If your guy is still unsure about asking you out, you can't just passively wait for him to get over his fear of asking you out. Going direct is an option, but you have to learn how to deal with rejection, whether implied or verbally expressed.

Some guys find it refreshing when a female asks them out. It saves them the agony of thinking up a good line. Boldness in dating is needed when you know for sure that some of the men around you will never get the courage to ask you out. Still, it's a fine line to walk because you must make sure that you ask him out without making him feel emasculated?

Try these tips that will help you make him feel more comfortable:

- **If he offers to pay, let him.** It doesn't matter if you are his boss or that you both know you earn more than he does. Offering to pay is a man's way of contributing to the date. Some men will never let a girl pay during a date, particularly the first one.

- **If a guy catches your eye at one point, acknowledge it with a smile or a friendly but questioning tilt of your head.** Pretending not to notice his effort to strike up a conversation with you will confirm his suspicions that you will not date him at all, even if he asked.

- **Let him choose the activity.** Suggest an activity that you think you will both enjoy, but ask him to pitch in a suggestion of his own so that he will feel like he had a hand in choosing the date's agenda.

"I'll *NEVER* Find the Right Person!"

When you are single, it can feel like you'll never find the right person, or any person for that matter. Then your friends ask you: "What have you done today to help yourself find the right person for you?"

The reality is that many women sit idly, only talking about the qualities they want in a guy, but not putting in effort to actually find one. There's no exact formula that you have to use to find the one for you; you simply have to use all available resources and explore all options within your vicinity.

Be open to new experiences. Don't immediately reject something that the rest of the world engages in to find dates. Does speed dating seem tiresome and pointless to you? You'd be surprised at how many people found true love in places that allowed singles to mingle. So give every opportunity a shot.

The first step to finding a date is admitting to yourself that you are looking to meet someone to talk to. The people you will meet don't necessarily have to fit your ideals, and you must take baby steps towards your goal of having a lasting relationship. Each one of the people who will approach you is unique. The key to finding a lasting relationship is self-discovery, and that begins when you find out what makes you really happy.

Chapter 10: Never Give Up On Love

Women often fear new relationships because they harbor the belief that past hurts will repeat themselves; to experience any new hurt is evidence of a never-ending cycle of hurt they are somehow destined for. People give up on love because it becomes a chore to analyze behaviors; it gets increasingly difficult go through the motions of falling in love and falling out of love, and most of all, nothing seems to work anymore.

The truth is that we tend to repeat old patterns in new relationships which can create these self-fulfilling prophecies, and this fear to open your heart again is exactly what keeps you from having the kind of healthy relationship that you're looking for.

You can learn how you can break the "pattern of failure" that seems to pervade each relationship you enter. Being single does not mean you have given up on love. In fact, there are many women are single and happy about it, too.

How to Break the Pattern That Leads to Relationship Failure

If all your relationships have been disappointing, you should analyze what you did, retrace your steps, and identify the patterns that you repeat whenever you start a new relationship.

Try to consider the following:

- **The environment wherein you met your ex-boyfriends.** Did you two meet in a bar? Were you slightly or more than a bit intoxicated when you met him? Did you meet in a neutral environment where anyone can strike up lively conversation? Did you immediately hook up right after you made eye contact? The places you frequent could tell a lot about the type of guy you will meet. In a bar scene, for instance, most will go there to check out other people and for one-night-stands. Your intention could be clean and absolutely wholesome, but the environment mostly only allows sexy dancing and hints of further nighttime mischievousness. Sure, they may be a few guys in these places who are looking for serious conversation about wholesome things, but the presence of alcohol skews things in favor of those who are there to have fun without thinking of long-term plans.

- **Your current emotional and psychological state when you started the relationship.** Women who are still recovering from bad relationships often fill the void they feel in their lives by engaging in another relationship right away without giving their selection process or their actions much thought. Being on the rebound means not dealing with current emotional crisis before plunging headlong in another relationship. Was your mindset focused on dating per se, or on finding a replacement fast?

- **Your idea of an attractive guy.** If you prioritize looks over personality or you don't get to know a guy well enough before committing, you are in big trouble. Women date the same type of guys and each time, each time believing that things will be different.

- **The point in your relationship when you start thinking about love.** What makes you decide that he is the one for you? Is there a point when you think he is into you as much as you are into him? There are many women who count the number of dates and give a deadline for the "chemistry" to happen. *"If we don't feel anything for each other on the third date, it's so over."*

- **Your expectations (whether expressed or not) when you started the relationship.** Simply put, you and your guy may not be on the same page when it comes to the definition of a long-term relationship. He could expect a "friends-with-benefits" relationship, while you expect a committed, monogamous one.

Once you have identified a pattern that you repeat over and over, you are well on your way to fixing your relationship attitude and starting anew. Giving up on finding love without trying to deviate from your own unique "failure patterns" seems like the easy way out, but not even trying to start over or being too proud to admit that the problem may be yours all along could result in a life of loneliness of thinking about what could have been and what-ifs.

Of all the dating mistakes, quitting is the worst one if you are still pining for that one guy to be your companion forever. Staying positive about yourself and your capability to change your patterns for the better is the key to finding the relationship that could make you happy.

Choosing to be Single and Being Happy About it

There are some women who have thought long and hard about their relationships and have decided to do away with all the mind games and the second guessing for an indefinite period of time. They choose to be single, not because they cannot get dates or they are fearful of dating, but because they have discovered that a committed relationship is not for them for the time being. After all, there is a difference between being alone and being lonely.

Being in solitude for a time, or indefinitely, does not mean that a woman is lonely. On the contrary, this time in a person's life can be used to regroup her emotions, rethink her dating strategy and just have fun being in non-committed relationships. Many singles are perfectly content that they don't have to go through the rigors of keeping up a relationship, particularly when their past ones have been less than satisfactory.

Women who decide to be single for a time need to be fully happy about their decision. No pining away for love, no incessant talks of ex-boyfriends, and definitely no "missing you" calls to exes who they hope will see the light about their past failed relationship with them.

"I'm not looking right now" is a powerful phrase, and those who say this with conviction have accepted that they need some time off from the turmoil that they have been through. Does this mean that they have stopped dating? Not necessarily. Consider it a hiatus from the grappling and the outmaneuvering that happens when people are looking to catch the crème de la crème of the opposite sex. If they do go out on dates, it's with the intention to have fun and not to find a suitable long-term mate.

TIME FOR MYSELF

If you have made the dating mistake of giving too much time to please another person, and forgetting to give something back to yourself, then a break from relationships is definitely needed. You don't need any more of that constant "must do this for him." You have all the time in the world to reflect about your strengths, what your former relationships taught you about life and love, and everything in between, not to mention your personal goals that probably took the back burner in favor of satisfying his needs. A wonderful single life is the time to be selfish without worrying about hurting someone with a self-centered approach to everything.

A lot of people turn out to be very good partners, parents, and friends after this "time alone." Sometimes the adjustments that we want in ourselves can only be realized when we take the time to look deeper into what makes us the way we are. Relationships are emotionally draining, and flitting from one to another in the blink of an eye can make anyone lose her perspective. Think of time off as time to breathe.

There are couples that manage to avoid an irrevocable break up by simply setting up a system that aims to give each partner personal time. Some regard it as giving each other time to "be single" again every once in a while. Think of this as a relationship sabbatical, that operates with the understanding that people need to know what they're missing to fully understand their roles as partners in a committed relationship. This time off is based on the cliché "If you love someone, set him free; if (s)he comes back, then it's meant to be."

KEEPING THE FAITH ALIVE, EVEN WHILE ALONE

Even those who have been disillusioned several times must keep the belief that they are capable of loving and that somewhere is a person who will appreciate the kind of love they offer. Take the time to be single to mend fences, patch up roofs, and straighten up the gate; much like the way a community rebuilds after a big storm. During this time, you can seek out your old friends whom you may have neglected during the time when you were busy with your most recent boyfriend.

Now is not the time to be bitter about your failures. It's the time to love yourself more. Most of all, this is the time to forgive yourself. Some people don't realize this important step in recovering from emotional trauma. There's always the nagging guilt that you have caused everything to break down in your former relationships. You need to identify the points that contribute to your guilt and address them one by one.

It helps to write a letter to yourself or someone very close to you and to simply pour out your heart. Keep a journal for daily realizations that you may have and read them all at once at the end of the week. You can start every sentence with "I just realized that…"

Be completely relaxed in your environment and avoid stressful things like jealousy over an ex's new relationship and thoughts of vengeance at being misled. Those things are all in the past, and now you can address them in such a way that you become honest with yourself completely.

- *Was I really a victim or did I do anything to worsen an already delicate situation?*

- *Did I overreact to everything like a desperate fish gasping for air?*

The good news is that you can tell yourself exactly what you feel without risking judgment, and every turn offers you the ability to forgive yourself and your ex-boyfriend(s).

Once you have a better sense of what you can offer a partner, you will have the renewed passion to date again. What matters now is that you stay positive about yourself. Time off is only good when you use it wisely. So catch up on everything that you missed while running around trying to please another person. Explore your world and discover things about yourself that you never knew existed.

And when you're ready, you can try again—when you're ready, and not before.